Sinful Pleasures

Sinful Pleasures

Sinful Ladies *of* London, Book One

KRISTI JUN

To Tricia,
Enjoy!
Kristi

BY KRISTI JUN

(Available in ebook and print)

REGENCY

Enemy's Kiss

THE SINFUL LADIES OF LONDON NOVELS
Sinful Pleasures, Book 1 (Now available on Amazon)
Sinful Kiss, Book 2 (Coming Soon)

ROMANTIC THRILLER

BAYROCK CHRONICLES
Jodi's Shadow, Book 1 (Coming Soon)

www.kristijun.com

For my husband and son. You are my world.

Prologue

St. Giles, London
February 1805

AMELIA KNIGHT WAS being sent away to Scotland for good.

In truth, her mother had never wanted her. Her mother, who'd been called a whore, preferred men over her own daughter.

Afraid and alone, ten-year-old Amelia hid in a corner of a dark, empty room above the tavern, sobbing. Within an hour, her grandmother's carriage would arrive to fetch her. She wiped her tears with her tattered sleeves.

A single candle lit the room, and she saw something move from the periphery of her vision.

"Look what I found." Millie Penn peeked out from under the bed and showed her the bread in her grimy hand, her mouth pulling to form a bright smile.

A sudden tug of sorrow held Amelia still. Millie had been her only true friend. "What do you mean, 'found'?" Amelia questioned, walking over to her.

Millie shrugged innocently.

"Did you steal from the bakery again?"

Millie crawled out of the tiny space. She nodded, and her dirty curls bounced. "I was hungry."

"You can't go stealing anymore, ye hear me?" Amelia said.

Millie nodded and wiped the dirt off her chin.

Amelia dug into a small inside pocket of her tattered, two-sizes-too-small coat and pulled out a silver shilling she'd been saving. She gazed at it longingly, then placed it in Millie's palm. "Don't let yer papa know you have it, ye hear?"

Millie took the coin and stared at it as if she'd discovered a pirate's booty.

Amelia sighed. "I have to go away."

Millie tucked the coin safety in her pocket. "Where are we going?"

"Not we," she said. "I . . ." She paused, suppressing the urge to cry again. "I'm going to Scotland."

"Sco-land?" Millie said curiously. "Where is that?"

"It doesn't matter where it is," Amelia said. "The point is, I have to go." The little girl's confusion was more than Amelia could bear. They'd always been together since Millie had been barely old enough to walk.

Smiling, Millie said, "Can I go with you?"

"No, Millie. You can't." No, Amelia would have to endure her awful grandmother for eternity on her own.

The little girl's mouth pulled together to form a pout, and tears formed in her eyes. "Who will play with me if you go?"

Amelia sighed again. Part of her wanted to be honest, but how would that help Millie? No, it was better that she didn't know the truth. "I won't be gone long," she lied. She knew she'd never set foot in London again.

"You promise?" Millie's big brown eyes sparkled with hope.

"Yes," Amelia said, halting the tears that wanted to spill. "Don't I always keep my promise?" The words barely made it out of her mouth. How could she tell Millie the truth— that she was never coming back?

The little girl nodded giddily, and she leaned into Amelia. Millie pulled the bread apart to share it with her. "Here, I saved you some."

Amelia looked at it, a hard lump forming in her throat and hot tears falling.

"Why are you crying?" Millie asked, confused. "I promise I won't steal again."

"It's not that."

Millie looked at her with her big brown eyes, waiting for a response.

"It's nothing," Amelia said, forcing a smile.

Taking a bite of her bread, Millie spoke while chewing. "You promise you will come back home?"

Amelia wiped away her tears and gave Millie a reluctant smile. "I promise."

Chapter 1

St. Giles, London
March 1815

AMELIA KNIGHT PULLED the hood over her head
and stepped into the mouth of hell.

The onslaught of familiar noises and the reek of the
slums paralyzed her when she stepped out of the carriage.
She looked around the outer limits of her surrounding for
signs of the rookery boys that had often roamed the streets
here when she was a child.

After ten years, nothing much had changed. The stench
of hunger and poverty still lingered thick in the air, bringing
back memories of her mum, her childhood. She quickly
dismissed them. Her mum might have wished a better
future for Amelia, but the reality was, the woman had never
written to her. Not a single letter.

"Are you sure you know what you are doing, Amelia?"
Kate McBride whispered, trailing behind her.

"Yes," Amelia said. "Just follow me." Kate, her good
friend, always loved adventure and would not allow her
to venture out alone. Kate had managed to commandeer

servants' clothes earlier today for this purpose, and Amelia didn't question where she had retrieved them from.

"Mrs. Pots will murder you if she discovers what we are doing."

Mrs. Pots, Amelia's chaperone for the Season and a loyal servant to Amelia's grandmother, would no doubt disapprove. Amelia's sole purpose for coming to London was to find a titled husband her grandmother approved of in order to gain access to her large inheritance—a temporary husband, of course, not that Amelia intended to tell her grandmother that—not to look for Millie Penn, her long-lost friend, at East End of all places. Her grandmother would find a way to make sure Amelia remained married permanently if she discovered what she planned to do once she inherited.

Her heart squeezed tightly. She'd promised Millie she'd come back, and now she had. In the loneliest of days when she was a child, Millie had kept her company and happy. Now, after all these years, she had plans for them both.

Once she found Millie, she needed to acquire a titled man who was desperate enough to agree to her plans. She had no intention of staying married. To anyone. Not if she had anything to say about it.

Amelia pulled off her gloves—it was easier to control the pistol that was safely tucked away in her reticule. "You are welcome to wait for me in the carriage, if you wish. There is a pistol under the seat should you run into any problems while I am gone."

Kate frowned in offense. "I am not about to let you do this alone."

They'd become fast friends in Scotland. The only reason her grandmother approved of their friendship was because Kate was wealthy—extremely so—and her late husband had a long lineage and was a part of Boston society.

Amelia looked at the ungodly looking creature with horns on the signpost that read "The Bull Tavern" dangling above the wooden door. Even before she entered the tavern, the door swung open fiercely, smacking against the brick wall. Soon, bursts of laughter shattered the silence and filled the quiet streets. She instantly took a step back, Kate right behind her. Her instinct was to run far from this unearthly place, but she remained still.

Two grungy men soon stepped out of the tavern. One wobbled side to side, tripped, and fell face-down on the cobbled street; the other man was obviously too inebriated to notice Amelia and Kate.

"Hand 'em over," the still-standing man said.

When the man on the ground didn't respond, the other man proceeded to kick the fallen man in his leg, shouting at him for the money he owed for the lady upstairs.

To Amelia's estimation, it went on for at least half a minute. When his attempt to collect the money proved unfruitful, he spat at the man and wiped his mouth with his dirty shirtsleeve. "Don't ye show yer face here again, ye hear." He grudgingly went back into the tavern without even noticing the women.

Amelia and Kate both unleashed their held breath, and Amelia felt the blood rushing to her limbs. As they neared the tavern door, a faint cry alerted her. Gooseflesh rose on her skin and her heart pounded in her chest. She heard it again, that haunting cry that had often crept out of her own mum's room and into the dingy hallway where Amelia used to play with Millie as a child.

She halted and listened carefully. *Sniff, sniff.*

Someone was most definitely weeping. "Do you hear that, Kate?"

"Hear what?"

"Over there," she said, pointing to the alley between the two buildings. "I am certain I heard a woman's cry." She took several steps, halted at the entrance of the alley and listened.

Sniff, sniff.

She took a deep breath and stepped forward into the dark passage, but Kate stopped her. "We don't know who might be lurking in there."

"She may need our help," Amelia said, still looking at the darkness. Kate was correct, of course. What good would it do to try to help if she ended up hurt or killed? How was that going to solve anything? Still, Amelia could not in good conscience leave the poor soul to suffer alone.

Amelia untied her reticule and pulled out her pistol for good measure, and both women proceeded to inch closer, looking into the alley. The faint light from the street lamp showed a silhouette of a small-framed person sitting slouched against the wall.

The weeping stopped.

Amelia froze. "Kate, stay here and keep watch."

"All right, but be quick," Kate said.

"Who's there?" a voice cried out from the darkness.

Amelia didn't want to frighten the woman, but time was of the essence. She put the pistol back in her reticule and moved closer.

"Stop or I'll scream," Amelia heard the woman say.

She halted. "I'm only here to help."

"Don't come any closer."

It was nearly impossible to see the woman's face from where Amelia stood, but one thing was very clear—she was with child. Perhaps this woman might know Millie and where she might be found.

"I am looking for Millie Penn."

The woman was awfully quiet for a moment, and Amelia held her breath. Did she have information that might be of use? Amelia prayed that she might.

"Why would I help ye?" the woman finally said, trying to stand. Her tone was bitter, resentful.

"I can pay you if that is what you desire."

No answer came from the woman. Amelia inched closer and saw her expression was one of lost hope, as if she had spent too many cold nights out alone in the dark, and her crestfallen expression, with her mouth cast downward as if she had had enough of this wretched life, was more than Amelia could bear.

The young woman touched her swollen belly, and her disheveled hair hung loose from the confines of her barrette. With her free hand, she pulled her frayed shawl over her shoulder and stood on her own two feet. "Wot do ye want with her?"

"She is a friend of mine," Amelia said. She swore she heard a cynical chuckle. Perhaps the woman did know, but didn't want to assist. Still, Amelia probed further. "Do you know where I might be able to find her?"

"*Psst*," Kate said from a distance. "I hear footfalls, so I'd hurry if I were you."

The young woman jerked back in fright as Kate walked up to them.

"It is all right," Amelia said to the frightened woman. But before she could soothe her, they heard the catcalls of the street gang approaching. All three women remained still.

"Can you walk?" Amelia asked.

"Yes," the woman said quietly.

"My carriage is not far . . . Here, this way." Amelia led the woman away from the cold brick wall. Beyond the alley, she heard the jeers and taunts of the street gang approaching. For heaven's sake, they didn't have much time.

"Do you think you can walk a little faster?" Kate asked.

Even with the pistol, Amelia was no match for brute force if her aim missed and the men decided to hurt them. They picked up speed and kept walking toward the street. The sound of boots slapping against the wet cobblestones paralyzed them. And before they could safely reach her carriage parked nearby, a deep voice shattered the silence in the alley.

"You've been a naughty woman, Miss Knight," said the voice, ripe with cynicism.

She felt her stomach drop. How did he know her name? She couldn't tell what the man looked like in the dark. Not that it mattered. She hadn't been out of her Mayfair townhouse more than a few times since arriving in London, and she hadn't been back in this part of London for over a decade.

The young woman slowly pulled away from Amelia and gazed at her strangely, as if she had seen a ghost. This was going to end very poorly if she did not soon figure a way out of this predicament.

Amelia turned and faced the tall, well-framed, hooded man several feet away. She quickly pulled out the pistol and cocked it. "Come any closer and I *will* shoot you."

He stopped dead, his face hidden by shadow. "I hardly think your puny pistol will do significant damage."

She'd never shot a pistol in her life, never mind held one. Kate had acquired the pistol and Amelia hadn't questioned it. "You can test your theory if you like." She forced herself to focus, despite the fact that she desperately wanted to run. "Either way, I will shoot, you can be sure of that." Was her voice trembling?

He observed them for a few seconds. "I doubt that," he said.

All three women inched backwards, step by step. "I have several Bow Street Runners on their way here as we speak. I will not be responsible for the outcome," she lied.

"Tsk, tsk, tsk. I don't think so, Miss Knight. I have eyes everywhere, you see," he said, gesturing with his hand. "This is my domain. You are all alone in this foolish endeavor to rescue a whore."

Her childhood memories flooded her like a torrid storm, slicing away what little courage she had left. Her mother had been a whore, that much she would not deny. She had watched as tyrannical men had dictated her mother's life and harassed her as if she were no better than property. Amelia would not succumb to such abuse by men, that she was certain of.

"Heed my warning," she said, pointing the pistol directly between his eyes. "I have known men like you . . ." She paused, forcing her own emotions down. "One more step and I *will* shoot to kill."

For a moment she thought she had won, but his mouth curved into a grin and her resolve diminished. "Rest assured I am not here for *that* kind of business. Not tonight anyway. I am here to deliver a message and take that bitch off your hands." He took a step closer. "You see, you have most defiantly inconvenienced my employer."

She dared not move, for if she did, she would likely try to shoot this horrible man and miss her target. "You tell your employer we will *not* be bullied by him, not as long as I am alive."

He paused and looked at her as though he were considering her words and their merit. An errant smile tipped the corners of his mouth.

Chills ran down her spine.

"Well then, we shall have to do something about that, won't we?" he said to her, and slowly approached...

Chapter 2

*T*HE STENCH OF *gunpowder and gore surrounded Richard, the Earl Blackthorn, as the ghostly white mist stilled like a thick blanket. In the distance, wounded men howled for help that would not come.*

Richard dropped to his knees, dug his fingers deep into the earth, and spooned fistful of dirt into his hands. Sweat and tears dripped down his cheeks like an endless dreary rain, grief clutching his heart. There was nothing he could do, not a damn thing; the man was already dead.

He slowly poured a thin layer over the dead man—enough to cover the body. The person he was burying was dead because of him. Without warning, the dead soldier opened his eyes, and his arms stretched out to grip Richard's neck. Richard pulled at the rigid, cold hands, but they felt like steel as he struggled to breathe.

"You did this," the soldier said, blood oozing out of his wounds and nose. Abruptly, the soldier's face morphed into Richard's dead brother, Max. "You did this to me!"

"No." He fought; each desperate breath became shallow, slowly pulling him deep into the

abyss . . .

Richard opened his eyes and gasped, his hands gripping his own neck. Air filled his lungs, his heart pumping away wildly in his chest. It was the damn nightmares again. Nightmares that had plagued him since his arrival in London.

The faint light of the lamp pierced the grimy window next to him, reminding him where he was—in his carriage on his way to visit Mrs. Bell, a widow with six young girls whom his brother, Max, had taken under his wing. His brother had been a good, honorable man with a soft heart for the less fortunate.

Ever since he'd returned home to London from his absence of nearly a decade, the eerie dreams had haunted him. And every damn time, he was reminded he should have been by Max's side when he was dying. Perhaps there was something Richard could have done to prevent his brother's death. But then again, he hadn't even known of Max's death until his mother wrote to him, urging him to come home.

Richard ran his fingers through the thickness of his hair in frustration and stretched out his legs. He detested London. There was nothing here to call home, he thought, looking out the grimy window again.

His father's passing several years ago had left the family with insurmountable debt from gambling and whoring. And his selfish mother continued to withdraw from the family's nearly empty coffer, spending her days in Bath in the comforting arms of her young lover.

His brother had inherited nothing of their parents' wicked character. Richard, on the other hand, had inherited his father's bad temper and his mother's penchant for avoiding people and large crowds. He chuckled to himself. His parents were rumored to have fallen madly in love, only to detest each other three years later to the point where his mother had left his father, permanently.

He ran his hand through his tousled hair again and let out an exhausted sigh. Leaning into the seat, he closed his eyes and listened to the clip-clopping of the horses' hooves and the occasional shouts of the residents nearby. The carriage jolted, and it sent a sharp sting through the joint in his shoulder—a knife wound he'd procured in his service to the crown. He'd seen enough of the human greed for power and money, enough corruption to last several lifetimes.

He was tired. He was done. There was only one reason for being in London: to close down the Blackthorn Estate and Somersby Hall and try to settle the debt to Sir Kendall his father had accumulated, then go hibernate somewhere quiet and retire. When he was dead and long gone, his cousin could inherit the damn properties and the title for all he cared. However, before all that could come to fruition, he needed to do one more thing for his dead brother. It was for his brother that he was making this visit to East End.

Within minutes, the carriage came to a full stop in front of an old bakery, its broken facade hidden by shadows. Being here brought a strange sense of wretchedness. Opening the door, he stepped out to the stench of rotten sewage.

Several feet away, he saw a gentleman's carriage parked

outside of the Black Bull Tavern. The driver was gone, which meant the carriage would be stolen in no time. The owner was going to be quite disappointed when he returned to find it gone; those steeds alone were valuable and could fetch a high price in London.

Above the bakery, a woman lived with six girls, all orphans. She and her husband had taken them in to prevent the young girls from turning to the whorehouses nearby. Now, with the husband dead, they were left destitute. Had he known sooner, he would have sent provisions for the widow and her girls.

He stepped over the open sewage flowing down the street and walked up to the door numbered ten. He knocked, then waited. It was late, and no doubt they were all sound asleep.

Soon, he heard movement inside the house, followed by light footsteps and a faint voice from the other side of the thin wooden door. "Yes?" he heard a woman say.

"Mrs. Bell," Richard said slowly, "I have a delivery."

No movement or sound from inside. He waited.

"A delivery?" she said from the other side of the door.

The shouts of drunken fools and a rabid dog barking across the street filled the silence. The door slowly creaked open just enough for him to see her thin face.

"From Mr. Maxwell," Richard informed her, hoping she'd let him in before the rookery boys took notice of them. It was the name Max had used when he became her patron.

"Mr. Maxwell," she said and quickly opened the door halfway, but didn't allow him inside yet.

Clearly, she could benefit from a good meal or two. She

was still young enough to remarry, but the darkness in her eyes looked as though she carried the weight of the world.

"I'm his brother, Richard," he said. The use of his Christian name seemed to suit better than announcing to her all his titles. Besides, his brother had addressed himself as Maxwell in his correspondence to Mrs. Bell and when he made his visits. "May I come in?"

She studied him for a bit, uncertain. Then she gazed past to the perimeter of the streets before she widened the door. "Please," she said, and allowed him to enter before she closed the shabby wooden door.

The dark room reeked of rotten vegetables and stale air. The woman quickly lit a single candle on the wooden table against the wall, and the dim light spilled into the small, crowded room. There, in the corner, he saw two little girls sleeping in a makeshift bed made of straw and a dirty blanket. This was no place for a widow and her six girls. He made a mental note to procure a more suitable place for them soon.

"Please," she said, gesturing to a wooden chair. "You are Mr. Maxwell's brother?"

Richard nodded as he sat on the flimsy chair. "Yes, I am."

"Then you must also know we are forever indebted to him." She pulled her tattered shawl up to her shoulders to warm herself from the chill. "We have not heard from him in so long. How is he?"

He cleared his throat as uneasiness crept into his heart. "My brother passed away not too long ago." Apparently, his brother had taken great care in making sure they received the provisions they needed after her husband died in the war. It was unclear how his brother had come to know this woman and her girls, but that was not his concern at the moment.

Instantly, her hand covered her mouth to stifle the shock. "I didn't know," she said, looking at him with sympathy burning in her eyes. "I'm sorry for your loss."

"Thank you," he said quietly.

"Your brother was a good man. I have never met a more generous man than he." She gazed at her daughter sleeping nearby. "It's a shame there aren't more like him."

The memories he'd buried pierced him. His father had said the same words to him of Maxwell: *a good, honorable man, a dutiful son.* Richard had always looked up to his brother for that very reason. "My brother found great joy in his patronage. But my loss, I fear, is naught compared to what you and your girls have had to endure since your husband's death. Tell me about the girls. How are they?" He had known the answer when he entered the house, but he felt it was polite to ask, nonetheless.

She nodded, wiping away her tears. "It has been very difficult," she said, looking at the little girl sleeping. "Beatrice is fifteen and very helpful. She's a serving girl at a tavern nearby and brings day-old bread on Fridays for the other girls. Olivia is thirteen," she continued, then paused as if a buried memory had resurfaced. She wiped her tears again and continued. "Georgette and Amanda are the closest in age, ten and nine, and they often help around the house, which is a blessing. Charlotte is over there, next to Francis." She stopped and looked at the small lumps on the makeshift bed. "They are good girls. I fear . . ."

Richard pulled out a small leather bag from his coat pocket. "Here," he said, handing it to her. "This should help."

The woman blinked several times, looking at the pouch with a mixture of disbelief and relief. She dabbed at her tears and let out a sigh as if a burden had been lifted from her shoulders.

"Not nearly enough, but it should assist you and your girls with food and whatever you need for a while."

Her gratitude was evident on her face. "You are most generous. I do not know how to thank you for this."

He recalled one of the letters from Mrs. Bell he'd found in his brother's drawer at Somersby Hall: *"If it hadn't been for you, I would have lost my girls to the godlessness of this place. I thank heaven for your generosity for saving their souls . . ."*

"It was my brother's wish, as it is mine, to do what we can." He stood. "Now, if you will excuse me, I must be heading back."

Just then something took hold of his leg and tugged at his trousers. He looked down and saw a little girl looking up at him with perfectly round, innocent eyes.

She yawned. "Are you Mr. Maxwell?" she said, wiping her eyes from sleep.

"No," he chuckled. "I'm afraid not."

"Mama speaks of him all the time, but she cries too. Are you here to help us?"

His heart clenched at her words. He reached down to pick her up and held her in his arms. "*He* was my brother," he said, and smiled at her. "What is your name?"

"Francis. You're handsome." She touched his cheeks

with her two tiny hands. "Isn't he handsome, Mummy?" she said, looking at her mother then back at him. "Are you married? Papa got sick and died and she needs a new husband."

He grinned wide and gently pinched her cheek—*such innocence*. "I think it is up to your mother whom she chooses to marry."

"Come," her mother said, reaching out to her. The little girl gladly bounced off Richard and clutched her mother. "Mr. Richard has to get on his way now."

He handed her his calling card. "If you need anything, don't hesitate to contact me."

She smiled.

He said his farewell and closed the door behind him. In a few months, he knew he would be gone from London and hoped never to return. Still, he felt he couldn't just leave without parting words to comfort her any way he could.

The carriage he'd seen earlier not far from the Black Bull Tavern, had a new owner now. The carriage raced by with mighty speed; a man inside stuck his head out and screamed at his accomplice to slow down. Damn fool for leaving the pricey carriage unattended in a place like this.

As he approached his own rented carriage, he saw a servant girl rushing toward him from the alley. She was frantically trying to get his attention. "There . . ." the woman said, pointing to the alley. "They need your help. Please." She begged him to come with her.

Bloody hell. He didn't need this now. "What is the matter?"

"Please, we need your help. My friend is in mortal

danger," the woman continued as she pulled at his sleeves, urging him toward the alley.

"Stay here," he said to the frantic woman. Richard quickly went in the direction she was pointing and stopped at the mouth of the alleyway. There he saw two servant girls, one held by the neck by a thug while the other pulled on his sleeves, begging him to stop hurting the other woman.

Amid her struggle, the hood fell off the captured woman's head and her long blond hair spilled down her back. A sudden primal need to protect her pulsed through Richard. He'd consider any man who laid a hand on a woman no better than a bloody animal that crawled the earth.

"Let go of me, you swine," Richard heard the brave woman shout at the man manhandling her. She kicked the cull on the knee, and he grunted in pain.

"Do that again and I shall have to break your neck," the brute said, still holding her in his grip.

"Mind your manners," Richard said, approaching.

The swine dropped the woman when she kicked him again. She managed to get some distance from the ruffian, but now he held the pregnant woman to him with a knife at the base of her neck. "Stop where you are, unless you want her death on your conscience."

Richard stopped and held both hands up to reveal that he had no weapon. "Why don't you do yourself a favor and release her?"

Richard looked at the angelic beauty next to him. His eyes raked over her full bosom in her bodice and her curves that put most women to shame. She'd be a target for rape in a place like this.

Shouts and laughter rang through the streets. From what Richard could tell, it looked to be the local street gang approaching.

The culprit slowly started to pull away deeper into the alley with the pregnant servant.

"This isn't over," the perpetrator said before briskly walking off with his captive.

Instantly, the blond woman tried to go after them and Richard stopped her. "You can't help her. Not now."

She desperately fought to get free of him, but she quickly realized she could not fight him on this.

"Are you all right?" he asked the woman. When she nodded, he continued. "My carriage is just around the corner. Your friend is waiting there for you."

Just then, all four of the rookery boys stepped out of the shadows.

Too late.

"I suggest you go," he said to her.

She looked back at him with confusion, her eyes questioning his demand. "But—"

"I said, go," he hissed, keeping his eyes on the men, "before it's too late."

"I cannot leave you here with them. How will you defend yourself?"

"Don't worry about me," he ordered, carefully watching the gang approaching.

She hesitated.

"Are you bent on getting both of us killed?" he hissed. "Now go."

The men inched closer. All four men were burly enough to do real damage. *Bloody hell, this is going to hurt.*

The blond woman handed him a small pistol. "You will need this."

He pulled out a large pistol hidden inside his greatcoat pocket. "Go," he said again.

She quickly scampered away.

The man who seemed to be the leader of the group gestured to the man on Richard's far left to follow the woman. "I don't think so," Richard said, quickly blocking his path.

"Whot ye goin' to do? Shoot us all?" the leader said. "Ye have only one pistol."

"Then I better make certain I do the most damage," he said, pointing the barrel of the pistol at the leader. "You're welcome to try to stop me, of course."

The leader narrowed his eyes and watched him carefully. "Yer not from 'round 'ere, are ye?" he questioned. "How's 'bout we make a deal . . . you and me, eh? Tell us where that pretty little woman yer hidin' is and we let you go."

"How about I shoot you instead?" Richard blurted out.

Just as he finished his sentence, he heard quick, light footsteps behind him, but he kept his pistol where it was.

"My aim never fails," a woman's voice said.

The angelic beauty stepped up to him and stopped. Their eyes met for the briefest of moments. His eyes followed the length of the barrel; it was pointed at the idiot's crotch. As angry as he was at her for putting herself in danger after he had saved them, a sudden burst of renewed energy surged through him, something he hadn't felt in a long time.

"But you're welcome to test my skill, if you so wish it," she said.

Who the bloody hell are you?

Chapter 3

AMELIA WAS AFRAID.

Very afraid.

Every fiber in her bones told her to run. But she couldn't. How could she? The stranger had risked his own life to save them. How could she leave him to fend for himself? With a quick glance at him from where she stood, she met his gaze. Those dark, steely eyes were intelligent and purposeful. She sensed an urgency in him to get away and flee, yet there was also an undeniable undercurrent of strength in him.

"We need to go," he said to her without taking his eyes off their would-be attackers.

In unison, she and the stranger slowly backed away. The rookery boys followed ever so slowly, matching their steps as if to surround their prey.

She noticed that the four men were mismatched. One man looked awfully young—no more than maybe sixteen. The one next to him looked to be missing a tooth when he grinned widely at her. One thing was certain; they all had a look that made her shiver with fright.

"Run," the stranger whispered, not taking his eyes off them.

"What about you?"

"I will be right behind you," he hissed. "Now go before you get us killed."

She hesitated for a second before she hitched up her skirt and ran toward the carriage that was parked nearby. Looking back, she saw the stranger right behind her. In that instant, she stepped on the hem of her skirt and fell forward onto the cold, hard cobble.

The slap of her cheek against the cold stone felt like a thousand knives. Just then, two strong arms swooped her up and she stood. Hand in hand, she and the stranger backed away, and once they escaped the alley, they ran as fast as they could to the carriage.

Catcalls punctuated the silence.

P-taff.

"Keep your head down," he ordered. They both ducked as they ran. Before she knew what was happening, she and the stranger were in the carriage. As soon as the carriage door slammed shut, it hitched forward and quickly picked up speed.

She slumped down on the seat and took a moment to catch her breath. She touched her raw cheek. Tonight had been one dreadful event after another. Instead of accomplishing her goal, she found herself in a precarious predicament, running for her life. And she could not help the poor pregnant girl. She feared what might happen to her in the hands of that horrid man in the alley.

Kate, who had been waiting for them in the stranger's carriage, shifted in her seat and Amelia started. She embraced her friend. "I am so glad you are all right, Kate."

"This, I fear, will have to be the last of my adventures for a quite a while," Kate noted, closing her eyes as she sank into the seat.

"You two have a strange way of defining adventure," the stranger remarked. "Reckless fits the situation, I'd say."

Amelia glared at him. There was some truth to what he said, but he didn't need to say it with such disdain. There was a sense of arrogance about him. He was heroic, yes, but still arrogant. She despised the word 'heroic.' Not because she didn't believe there were men of such traits, but because the idea often gave one a false perception of reality.

Reality was far too cruel.

Then there was her chaperone who had thus far managed to ruin every fiber of hope she had managed to gather in her spirit. If Mrs. Pots discovered her secret plans to annul the marriage and live out the rest of her life in peace of her own free will, she would no doubt inform Amelia's grandmother at once and hence deprive her of her inheritance. After all, Mrs. Pots had been loyal to her grandmother for nearly two decades. She had been given precise orders to make certain Amelia didn't stray from her grandmother's wishes, and Mrs. Pots was only too happy to oblige.

Amelia's eyes met the stranger's and, in that instant, there was an immediate attraction she could not deny. His gaze felt like someone had reached into her chest and gripped her heart, and she felt her blood pumping wildly through her veins. His chiseled features, those dark tousled curls that framed his handsome face. No, he wasn't just handsome, but rather striking. He was . . . well, a cut above the rest to say the least. And now, the way he looked at her made her want to jump out of her skin. But there was something else about him that was somber, too. Reserved, stubborn, and somber, she thought curiously, and for a single moment she wondered what had happened to him.

Stop this nonsense, she chided herself. Her inquisitive mind was never a good thing, and she didn't like this feeling. This attraction was unreliable and fleeting, and it would get her into more trouble than it was worth. And she had learned that lesson well. One that she did not plan to repeat.

Amelia shifted in the confined space. "Where are you taking us?"

His brow lifted, and his mouth twisted. "You are not a prisoner."

She felt foolish. That was not what she meant. "I am aware of that." She sighed in frustration. "Mayfair number ten." It was not number ten, but rather twelve, but he didn't need to know that either.

His mouth pulled in displeasure. "Do your employers know you skulk about in East End without regard to your safety?"

Kate quickly nudged her not to respond to his comment. Amelia looked up and saw the stranger looking at her again. He had a perplexed expression on his face, maybe even amusement.

No, she was not a servant. In fact, she was an heiress

who would inherit tens of thousands upon a marriage to the man her grandmother approved of. But then this stranger had no business in her private affairs either.

"I would be much obliged if you didn't question my affairs, Mr...?"

He frowned. "Waters."

Interesting. He didn't look like a Mr. Waters—not that she knew what a Mr. Waters should look like. "Thank you," she said. "And . . . thank you for your assistance."

"I didn't have much of a choice," he said, closing his eyes.

How rude. Again, Kate nudged her to not get involved, so she kept her mouth shut. No matter. Soon, she would never see this rude man again.

Everything went silent inside the dark carriage for several minutes and she was thankful for it. Still, even in the dimness of the carriage, she felt his eyes on her. She shifted, and their knees touched. This confined space was starting to annoy her a great deal, and she kept looking out the grimy window to see if they were close to her destination.

"It was foolish of you to come to a place like this alone."

"I wasn't alone. I had a friend and my pistol."

"Neither of which were helpful."

"I thank you for your assistance, Mr. Waters, but I would like it if you kept your opinion to yourself."

"It's clear someone has to talk some sense into you," he blurted out. "These men won't think twice before taking liberties with women."

She'd been lectured to for the last decade. She'd disliked it then, and she certainly didn't like it now. "You needn't preach to me. I am quite aware of the dangers."

He muttered something to himself, then the stranger eased back into his seat. She felt the tension drip away slowly. Thank goodness. If she were lucky, he'd leave her be the rest of the ride home to Mayfair. She wasn't a fool and was quite aware of how dangerous it was going to be for her, but she had no other choice in the matter. She had promised Millie she'd return.

In the last decade, two letters from Millie had slipped through her grandmother's fingers. One had arrived nine years ago, and the second letter a year ago. Millie had made no mention of her mother, just the crumbling situation she was living in. Amelia had sent some provisions and money through Kate, but since then, she hadn't heard from Millie again. It was then she had known she must do something to help her. After all, Millie was a childhood friend; Amelia had even considered her a little sister.

The light from the street lamp splashed into the carriage and she caught a glimpse of the man's face again. He was looking at her rather strangely, as if she were a thing to be studied under his scrutiny. There was intelligence in those eyes and his face . . . well, it was a sin to look the way he did. Positively sinful. Not mention *rude*.

Her gaze lowered to his finely formed cravat and his clothing donned in refined gentry. She knew she should look away, but she felt intoxicated by the lure she felt for this man. She'd never known herself to be this entranced by a man purely from his appearance, but there was something about him deep beneath those eyes of his.

Another flash of light spilled into the carriage, this time for a few seconds longer. Her gaze lowered to his broad shoulders, then to his well-muscled legs that filled his breeches well. Her gaze swooped up and met his again, and her heart leaped.

Amelia averted her gaze, not wanting to give away anything she wasn't willing to. When she thought he wasn't watching her, she peeked over and saw him look out the grimy window as if contemplating something.

Familiar streets of Mayfair alerted Amelia. Everyone remained silent and she was thankful for it. Tonight had been so filled with one disaster after another that she hadn't even considered how she was going to find Millie now, given tonight's unsuccessful venture. She had planned for every detail, but what had transpired tonight was not part of the equation. She needed to think.

When the carriage slowed, she saw a row of townhouses on Upper Brook Street. The carriage jerked and stopped. From where she was, she could imagine that dreadful Mrs. Pots pacing her carpet. She was like a hawk that never slept, reporting her every move to Amelia's grandmother, that dreadful woman.

She must have looked worried, because the next thing she noticed was the man in front of her, watching her.

He said, "I doubt she'll notice if you sneak in from the mews."

She bit her lower lip, thinking about what she should say. Kate had already stepped off through the other door, gesturing for Amelia to join her.

"I suggest you take off your shoes first."

30

Why didn't she think of that? "Thank you," she said, stepping off the carriage when he made no attempt to help her down. Why should he, when he thought she and Kate were only servants? Before she could say another word, he shut the carriage door and ordered the driver on.

Clearly, he didn't care to be in their presence.

When the carriage was nearly out of sight, Kate said, "Delicious and heroic, isn't he?"

"And rude," Amelia retorted.

"Well, we did inconvenience him, didn't we?"

"If you say so. Let's get inside before someone notices we are missing."

They quickly walked down the stairs that led to the kitchen and servants' quarters, and Amelia slowly opened the door. She pulled her shoes off, and Kate followed suit without any comment.

In the dark, they speedily made their way through the kitchen and up the servants' stairs to the second floor where Amelia's room was located. Kate bid her goodnight and slipped into her room. Amelia's room was near Mrs. Pots', so she tiptoed to the room, avoiding the spots where the floor squeaked. When she was safely ensconced in her room, she exhaled.

In the dark, she hastily undressed and slipped under her blanket. Her mind ran wild, replaying the events of the night, including the stranger who had saved them. That insistent, insufferable, gallant man who'd had the courage to face danger and come to their rescue. She wondered who the man was for the umpteenth time.

No more than five minutes later, her door creaked open and a shadow appeared: *Mrs. Pots.* The woman lingered there for several seconds before she closed the door again. Amelia frowned. *That* woman. She had known Mrs. Pots long enough to predict her actions. The blasted woman didn't allow for any privacy, walking in and out of Amelia's room as if she owned the place.

As annoyed as she was, it was late, and she needed to get some sleep. She doubted she would be able to, but she tried nonetheless. But even before a full minute had passed, thoughts of Millie came to her. She hoped to God she would find Millie soon. It would take a miracle. Did she even believe in such a thing? Knowing she didn't, she felt her heart sink as she closed her eyes.

Earl Blackthorn closed his eyes and smiled as the rented carriage drove off after delivering the women to the Mayfair townhouse.

They had the audacity to present themselves as scullery maids. Hmm, he didn't know where they had acquired the clothes, but he knew for certain they were no servants. Call it a hunch, and the very fact that these women had on very expensive pairs of silk shoes. Then there was their speech. The stolen carriage might have belonged to them, too. He'd been trained to notice even the most minute details as a spy for the Crown. Now retired, he'd thought he was done with such dubious activities.

Light from a street lamp streamed into the carriage and

he saw something twinkle in the light before going dark again. Leaning forward, he grabbed it. The small ornate pouch felt like silk between his fingers. One of the women must have left it in the carriage in her haste to get back inside their townhouse unnoticed.

They were bloody hell reckless. Not even he would choose to go to East End in the middle of the night. Who were these bloody women? And why the hell were they skulking about in a place like Whitechapel?

"The damn bloody whore," Sir Andres Kendall said, pulling off his black wig and tossing it on the desk in his study. That was a close one. He had had enough of Millie causing trouble in his life and now the chit, Amelia Knight, was vexing him. Tonight, he made a decision. He could no longer afford to have the whore running about causing trouble.

A knock on the door alerted him. *Who the hell is it now?*

Philip, his only child, peeked into his father's study. Quickly shoving his wig into the bottom drawer, he waved his son into the study.

"Father, is everything all right?" Philip walked into the study and stopped in front of his father's desk, worry etched on his face.

"Of course I am all right," Kendall said to his idiot son. His curly red hair and constitution resembled his late mother. The only thing he seemed to have inherited from his father was his height of six feet and one inch.

"When you didn't attend the dinner this evening, Lady

Lucinda and I became worried."

Damn, Kendall had forgotten about the dinner. His presence at East End had been a last-minute decision, one that he could not put off any longer. "I had matters to attend to, son, but rest assured, everything is all right."

"Good," Philip said, smiling.

Philip's soon-to-be fiancée, Lucinda, was a budding beauty of the *ton*, and the third and youngest daughter of the Earl Hallwickton. At age seventeen, the brown-eyed beauty had taken a liking to Philip when they were introduced at a dinner party earlier that month. Kendall knew it would be a perfect opportunity to be connected to a title and long heritage, something he had often dreamt of since his son's birth.

"I must make my apologies to the earl."

"You are in luck, Father. I told the earl you had taken ill and retired for the evening," Philip said, smiling wide. "If all goes well, I shall be asking for her hand in marriage, and I didn't want any misunderstanding between the families."

Kendall smiled in approval. For once, his son had learned something. This was a good sign. A good sign indeed.

When he'd seen Millie resting against the wall in the alley, sobbing and caressing her swollen belly, he'd known he was in luck. He'd been contemplating what to do with the whore when the two bitches showed up, causing him to hide in the dark.

Now that Millie was locked away in the attic of his townhouse, she wouldn't be causing any more problems. He'd figure out what to do with the chit soon.

Chapter 4

AFTER TWO HOURS of attempting to sleep, Amelia sat up in her bed and lit the candles on the candelabra on the nightstand next to her bed. With all the excitement tonight, how could she possibly sleep? Being in London, after a decade of absence, brought back so many memories of her mother and Millie.

Memories that burned with resentment and sadness.

Amelia touched the silver necklace around her neck and stroked the stone with her fingers, memories flooding back to her:

"Please, Mummy, I don't want to live with that woman." *Her grandmother blamed her mother for everything, including her father's death. Or at least that was what she'd been told by Cook, who was a kind man who let her mummy cry on his shoulders and let Amelia have leftovers in the kitchen when she was too hungry to sleep.*

"Hush," Amelia's mummy said. "That woman you speak of is your grandmother. You'll have everything you'll ever want in

this world."

"I don't want to go to Scotland," Amelia said. "I want to stay with you."

The shouts of laughter and sound of shattering glasses from below caught them off guard. For several seconds, they remained frozen, listening. When quietness engulfed them again, she looked back at her mother.

"Look around you," her mother said. "Is this what you want?"

Amelia looked around the dim, narrow hallway. This place wasn't so bad if she had her mum and Millie. She looked at her mummy again—she always looked so tired . . . so sad.

Her mother lowered herself to her knees and looked squarely at her. Amelia saw tears forming in her mum's eyes and it began to worry her. Taking off her silver necklace, her mum gazed longingly for a moment at the shiny green stone dangling there.

"Here," her mummy said, putting the necklace on Amelia.

Wide eyed, Amelia touched it with her hand. Her mother never took it off, so why was she giving it to her now? A swell of emotions filled her, as if somehow her mum were making a final gesture.

"You need to go."

Amelia felt a lump in her throat and she couldn't stop the hot tears from falling. "No, Mummy."

"You must," her mother said firmly. "Be strong, you hear me?"

Amelia nodded, touching the cold silver necklace around her neck. She felt a sudden urge to hold on to her mummy and never let go.

"Let no man, no matter who he is, dictate your life. Promise me."

Amelia wiped the tears from her eyes. She understood now why she had been sent away, yet anger and resentment burned in her heart every time she thought of her mother. Partly because of her mother's lack of interest in her life and the fact that she'd never attempted to visit her.

She touched her necklace again, thinking she should really remove it, but no matter how many times she tried, she couldn't. It had been on her neck for a decade, and despite the painful memories, she didn't have the heart to remove it. Besides, it reminded her what she needed to accomplish here in London.

That wasn't the worst of it. Her grandmother was an angry woman and Amelia couldn't understand why. She had been told again and again how her mother had caused her father's death, but her grandmother had said nothing else to elaborate on the accusation when questioned. Because of the son taken away from her, her grandmother had tasked Amelia with making certain she married a respectable man from a proper family with a title. She'd been bred for this purpose.

Thoughts of the stranger materialized in her mind. An introduction would have been proper, at least, but with everything happening so fast, she hadn't thought of it until now. Did it matter?

For a moment she allowed the romantic notion of the stranger to play out in her mind. Silly, she knew. In a perfect world, she dreamt that he was honorable and strong, and stood for all that was good in this world. She chuckled inwardly at the blind stupidity that still seemed to plague her.

While he may have rescued her and Kate, there was a sense of gravity about him. Maybe even gloom? She wasn't certain why or how, but she sensed it.

Amelia pulled off the blanket, stepped off her bed, and walked across her room to her desk. There atop a stack of unopened letters sat a parchment containing the list of eligible bachelors in London.

Picking it up, she looked at the list with trepidation. She had folded and unfolded this parchment more than a dozen times since she had arrived in London two weeks ago. And each time she read the names, it ate away the courage she had built up before coming to London. Sickened by the thought of becoming chattel, she braved the list of names again:

Lord Benedict Rowland Grayson
Lord Richard Nickolas Blackthorn
Lord Henry Adam Fletcher

All titled men of impeccable breeding with long prestigious heritages. Grandmamma had reminded her before leaving for London that these men would have no reason to deny her if she conducted herself appropriately and abided by Mrs. Pots' instructions. Her grandmother's words were: *These men expect to marry a lady of good breeding. I require you to conduct yourself as such—a lady. Mrs. Pots will be reporting to me on all accounts of your conduct.*

Even in her ill health, Grandmamma was ordering her about. Her grandmother's personal physician had informed her that she could not travel to London with her weak heart.

Amelia was thankful for it; not that her grandmother was ill, but that it gave her the opportunity to carry out the plan she'd had in mind since arriving in Scotland a decade ago.

Her inheritance would be most beneficial to the men of the list and their carefully selected families. But if these families discovered the truth about her birth, they would surely have reservations about the marriage, and that would mean an end to her carefully formulated plan—her plan to be rid of men for good, to live out her life as she deemed fit without orders, without schedules, until her last breath.

Amelia was tired of schedules and tired of pleasing others. She knew all too well that men looked upon their wives as property and treated them as they deemed fit. She told herself she would not allow men, or anyone else, to dictate her life, and she told herself she would gain her freedom one day. If she remained married, she would not have that freedom. Men only wanted her for her inheritance and to control her, as her grandmother did. The only way to ensure her survival was to make sure no man had control over her life and her own funds.

She wasn't about to be confined to rules set by Society, only to live and die by them. She had other plans. *Two months*. Just two short months to find out which one of these men was desperate enough to agree to her terms of marriage—or business transaction, rather. Perhaps Lord Blackthorn. With some digging, she'd discovered he had inherited a substantial debt. It would be difficult for him to say no to her proposal. If the debt were called and he couldn't pay, he'd face debtors' prison and shame.

Amelia sat on the edge of her bed, not moving. For a single moment, she allowed her mind to wander to a place she rarely allowed herself to go—her mother. It wasn't that she hated her, no; it was deeper, more complicated than that. She had written to her mother for months, but when no reply came, she had finally come to realize that her mother had no interest in staying in touch and, according to her grandmother, her mother wanted nothing to do with Amelia. After a decade, Amelia had had no knowledge of her mother's whereabouts at all. And in all truth, she'd rather not know.

She shook her head when emotions brewed inside. Goodness, she'd promised herself she would not do this to herself. Her goal was to find Millie, a promise that she couldn't break. Millie had somehow managed to write to her, and it was by sheer chance she'd gotten her hands on the letters. Her heart stung at the memories.

The letters were short. Millie hadn't spoken of her mother. Only mentioned she'd never forgotten about their friendship and that she missed Amelia terribly. She'd also mentioned her father, who had beaten her so badly at one time that she'd run away from home for nearly two weeks. When she'd returned, he'd tossed her out of the house and told her never to come back unless she had money to contribute.

This news had brought Amelia much pain. This was when she'd resolved to help Millie, to find her and keep her promise. She surmised her own childhood would have been unbearable without Millie. She let her tears fall. They trickled down her cheeks, allowing her to sob away the pain she kept deep in her heart and hidden from the world.

Several minutes later, in the quiet of her room, her thoughts turned to the handsome stranger again. She thought of what might have happened to her, Kate, and the young woman in the alley had he not intervened. She knew very well the dangers that lurked in the streets of St. Giles. But tonight had ended terribly because she couldn't help the poor young woman, whoever she was. She could only hope the young woman would not suffer too much. Deep in her heart, Amelia knew it was a fruitless optimism.

She plopped back in bed and closed her eyes. The self-assuring magnetism of the stranger who had rescued them intrigued her, more than was good for her, and she felt childish lying on her bed thinking about the brave gentleman she was never going to meet again.

During the ride back, she'd had a good deal of time to observe the stranger, and she'd guessed he didn't lack women's company. Probably had an inflated ego, too.

She pulled the soft pillow to her and hugged it. She surmised she was so fascinated with the man because it distracted her from her current troubles. Deep loneliness engulfed her again. Kate's friendship was a blessing, but this feeling was different. Sometimes, the isolation she felt in the evenings was unbearable.

Chapter 5

"OH, GOOD, YOU have arrived." Blackthorn's mother, the Countess Blackthorn, whom he hadn't seen in many years, stood up from the settee near the hearth in his study.

His initial reaction was shock and confusion, followed by acute annoyance. He gave her a sidelong glance of utter disbelief, and she frowned in return. His so-called mother had returned after nearly a decade of absence as if nothing had transpired within the family.

"Darling, is that how you greet your own mother?"

For the first time in his life, he was utterly speechless. He watched her stand and saunter over to him. Good God, she was swathed in gold and diamonds. Her dress alone could feed a household, and that diamond necklace could feed a country. Her husband had managed to empty nearly half of the family coffers, and his mother was depleting what was left of it.

She began, "I am aware I have been . . . absent—"

"Try for a decade."

She held back a frown. "Now, son. I had a reason for being away so long, you know this," she said matter-of-factly.

The reason being Blackthorn's father and her dreaded husband, who was now dead. A man she chose to marry and then abandoned. And now that he was dead, she was free to return from Bath.

"Where is that manservant of yours?" Blackthorn wasn't about to use her lover's name. Her lover only remained with her because she lavished him with anything he desired. He could hardly believe his parents had once professed undying love for each other.

She waved her hand in the air as if it were nothing of consequence. "I desired him gone."

"Just like that?"

She frowned. "Your father had three lovers that I know about. After I gave him two sons, I left. It was what he desired."

Memories of the shouting and bickering all those years at Blackthorn Hall was enough to make Blackthorn pack up his things and leave the county. It had been rumored that he was a bastard child because of his black hair. No one in his family possessed black hair and blue eyes, but there was no solid proof to back up the rumor, and his parents had squabbled about it without end.

But no, he was here at the wish of his brother, who had wanted him to resolve their father's debt, release the servants, and close down the house. He would honor that promise. His brother had cared about the honor of their family name. Richard didn't. His brother had always been thoughtful and had written to him as much as he could while he was away at war. This was the least Richard could do for him. It pained him that he hadn't been there when Max passed. Perhaps that was the reason for the nightmares, the guilt eating away at him. He'd come home as soon as he heard of his brother's condition.

After Richard's death, the earldom would be passed on to his cousin, or whoever was next in line, because he wanted nothing to do with the title. The title and the land were more trouble than they were worth. There was nothing here that he wanted. Nothing here that brought memories he cherished. For all he cared, his mother could go wherever she pleased as she had always done.

"Why are you really here?" he said. "Have you already managed to spend the thousands of pounds father gave you?"

"How dare you speak to me as such. I am still your mother."

He held back a retort. He was tired and wanted to be done with this. As far as he was concerned, she has no right to speak to him about anything, period. The woman had left him while he was at Eton when he'd been eight. She came back twice, just twice, once when he was fifteen, and the last time when he'd been nearly twenty. She had stayed only a few hours each visit before returning to Bath. Max had been an emotional child, and it had been hard on him to watch his mother go. Richard, on the other hand, couldn't wait for her to leave, as she only brought them grief.

"If you must know, I came home to see you."

Another lie. "That is hard to believe." She actually had the nerve to look pained by his remark. "I don't plan to stay long and your presence here is not needed. I am going to bed." He started to walk away, but stopped. "I prefer you remain at Blackthorn Hall, as this is my private residence." He'd purchased this townhouse when he'd been spying for the Crown and worked for Home Office.

"What do you mean you don't plan to stay long? What about the estate?"

"What about it?"

"You are the Earl Blackthorn now. You have responsibilities."

Just then, there was a knock at the door. Who the hell was it now? "Come in."

A woman in her mid-twenties, donning a gray dress, entered. "My lord." She curtsied. "My lady, your bags have been delivered to your room. And the bath is ready. Is there anything else you require of me?"

"Bath at this hour?" he blurted out.

"I have been traveling all day."

"Good night," he said, and started to walk to the door.

"Just a moment," his mother said to him, forcing him to wait as if she had a dire situation she needed to remedy. "Has my cook arrived? And what about my butler?"

The young maid, still standing there, said, "Yes, they arrived an hour ago, my lady."

"How many servants did you bring with you?" Blackthorn asked.

"Just what I need."

Bloody hell. "You will remove your staff from *my* house first thing in the morning to Blackthorn Hall." He kept a minimal staff of three servants on purpose, and she'd brought a town with her.

"If you insist on it. But before I depart, I would like to inform you Elizabeth is in London."

He hadn't heard that name in years. She had made her choice when she ran off with that bloody goat. "And?"

"Elizabeth was saddened to heard about Max . . . and your father, too."

"How good of her," he said dryly. "How's the earl?"

His mother observed him most curiously before she spoke. "You haven't heard, have you?"

"Heard what?" There was an edge to his tone he didn't like.

"Her husband . . . he passed nearly eleven months ago."

So, the old goat was dead and now she schemed to get her claws in him, was that it? When he wasn't titled, she had wanted nothing to do with him. "If the countess's company brings you some measure of comfort, don't let me stop you." His mother was naïve about the self-serving widow.

"My dear boy, it's not my happiness I am concerned about." She paused, perhaps waiting for him to respond. When he didn't, she continued, "Indeed, it would make me happy if you thought about marriage."

To that self-serving woman? "Let me remind you that you have no say in what I choose to do with my life." When his mother looked as though she was about to argue his point, he said, "It's late."

"I invited her to the ball," she quickly said.

This just kept getting better and better. "The ball?"

"The Blackthorn Ball, of course."

"I have told you, I don't plan to stay long." There would be no expense of a grand ball this Season; he didn't give a damn what Society thought. He watched his mother's expression. She had the audacity to look appalled at his response. His patience was growing very thin. "So that there is no misunderstanding between us, I am here for Max. It was his last wish to settle Father's accounts, and once that is accomplished, I will be leaving London for good."

She looked astounded. "What do you mean, 'for good'?"

"I am closing down the estate, releasing the servants, and leaving." He would sell Somersby Hall, and once he got an offer, he'd pay off the debt. His brother had purchased the property with building a family in mind, but with him gone, there was no need to keep it. Max had said Blackthorn Hall had too many dreadful memories.

"You cannot do this," she said. "What will people think?" She meant who would take care of her and her extravagant lifestyle.

"We have a summer cottage in the country. You will have an allowance." He didn't bother to wait for a response. He snatched up the correspondence on his desk, locked up his ledger book in the drawer, and walked out of the study, leaving her standing there with her mouth open. For a mother who hadn't shown up for her own son and husband's funerals, it was what she deserved.

As he walked down the hall and up to his room, Blackthorn made a mental note to send the mystery woman a note in the morning, telling her where she could collect the reticule she had left behind in the carriage.

His thoughts turned to the blond woman with curiosity. He'd didn't want to think what might have happened if he'd not been there to assist. Although she had the courage to defend herself, she had been in no way prepared for the gang of murderers and thugs that roamed the streets. Foolish woman.

One by one, he went through the stacks of missives and invitations to the upcoming balls and dinners that fell onto his desk like a waterfall. As he went through them, a letter from his solicitor caught his attention, and he dropped the rest of the stack on his desk. Good, perhaps he had some good news about Somersby Hall.

Quickly, he broke the seal and read the contents, letting out a long sigh of relief. He read the one-paragraph note carefully, then once again. A wide smile crept onto his face and the burden he'd been carrying seemed to slowly melt away—finally, an offer for Somersby Hall. The last potential buyer had changed his mind, leaving Blackthorn to doubt that anyone wanted it at all.

This would surely put his father's debt to rest. He read on . . .

The prospective buyer was Miss Amelia Knight. Familiarity slowly sank in. The pouch he'd found in the carriage had a calling card with the same name engraved on it.

Hmm. . . His interest was piqued. Was she the heiress? The richer the better because, in all truth, he needed a fortune.

Richard awoke while it was still dark, drenched in sweat and gripping his throat.

It took him a moment to figure out where he was. Same damn nightmares. They had started when he heard the news of his brother's death. The damn guilt was eating at him even while he slept.

Pulling off the blanket, he put on a robe and opened his window, allowing the chilly breeze to cool him. The domestic life thus far was proving to be more difficult than he had originally thought. He felt this unnerving urge to run. He felt like he couldn't find his footing and was sinking deeper and deeper into the unknown.

Closing the window, he pulled on his breeches, shirt, and thick outer coat. Not bothering with the cravat, he slipped an Indian Jambiya dagger inside his coat pocket and walked out of his room.

Soon, he stepped out into the streets of Mayfair.

His warm breath surrounded him. Pulling his collar up, he yanked the coat tightly around him against the chill and walked into the darkness.

He didn't know where he was going.

And he didn't care.

He just needed to leave, get away from this place.

Chapter 6

T HE BREAKFAST TABLE in the morning room shook when Mrs. Pots planted the parchment on the table, nearly spilling her coffee over the rim of her floral china.

"What is this?" Amelia said, trying her best to restrain herself from telling Mrs. Pots exactly what she thought of her behavior.

"You know exactly what this is," Mrs. Pots noted. Her hands were perched on her hips.

The middle-aged woman's hair was pulled back so tightly in a topknot, Amelia feared it would snap. And her drab-colored dress made her eyes look even darker, like death coming to claim its prize. "You have exactly thirty minutes to start your lesson." With these words, her chaperone swiftly left the room.

"My, my . . . such a ruckus so early in the morning," Kate said, sipping her coffee. "The woman really needs a good tupping, if you ask me."

"Kate," Amelia whispered across the table. "She might hear you."

"Good," Kate said, setting the cup down. "I wouldn't mind telling her exactly what's on my mind for once."

"You know we can't risk Mrs. Pots reporting back to Grandmamma." Amelia fought hard against the anger of being denied the simplest of things by her grandmother.

"The woman thinks you are still ten years old." Kate inhaled deeply. "Honesty, Amelia, you are nearly twenty-one, and yet the woman has you taking lessons on French verb conjugation, not to mention a myriad of other useless lessons you have to endure each day."

"My grandmamma arranged all this to keep me occupied and in the grips of Mrs. Pots' control. It is what I must do, for now." Once she'd been locked up in her room for days after a lashing for refusing to do the lessons. Mrs. Pots had informed her grandmother that Amelia was an impossible child who simply would not conform to the rules set before her. She would have been more than happy to run away, only the woman seemed to find her one way or another. In the end, she had decided to pay the price of complete obedience for the remaining years until she received her inheritance. Only then would she live freely without any attachments, as *she* saw fit.

"I know, my dear friend," Kate said softly. "I just wish you could have more fun while you are in London."

"I do, too."

"Perhaps if we were to procure Mrs. Pots a hobby, she won't have the time to dictate your every action." Kate raised her brows and smiled widely to lighten the conversation. "Shall I arrange it?"

"That would help my cause." The truth was, Kate's candid comments and perspective in life were quite refreshing. Perhaps because Kate's life was so dissimilar to Amelia's. As an American, she tended to say what was on her mind, and being a widow, she had the life experience to take chances. Amelia was thankful for their friendship, especially since she didn't make friends very easily.

Her thoughts drifted back to the predicament at hand. There was so much at stake that sometimes she felt unable to breathe for fear of making an error. If her chaperone discovered her plans and informed her grandmother, she would lose her inheritance, and with it, her future plans to be self-sufficient and unattached.

"So, what's in the schedule for today?" Kate said, breaking Amelia's thoughts.

With a sigh, she picked up the parchment and read it out loud:

11:00 AM: Read three chapters of On the Proper Conduct of a Genteel Woman and conjugate verbs in French (the lesson is on your desk)
1:00 PM: Light lunch
2:00 PM: Stroll at Hyde Park
4:00 PM: Tea and reading of Proverbs 2:7 and 2:8 (discuss in detail the virtues of the upright)
5:00 PM: Meet with modiste for a final fitting of the dresses
8:30 PM: Lord Grayson's Ball

"I just wish I could have one day to myself, is all."

Kate looked as though she was thinking of something clever to say. "Shall we escape the evil queen and stop by Bond Street for some shopping? Perhaps a visit to the confectioner's to put the smile back on your face?"

"That sounds delightful, but you know I can't." Amelia had written to the seller's agent about Somersby Hall two days ago and had not heard back from the agent. She hoped the property wasn't sold. She had seen the idyllic place when she first arrived in London and immediately thought of Millie. Nestled in the hills in the outskirts of London, it had a small lake behind the property, and trees. Lots of trees. Perhaps oak, she wasn't certain, but she knew it was perfect.

She hadn't discovered it was on sale until Kate mentioned that the owner, who happened to be one of the names on the list of bachelors she was to consider for marriage, was entertaining offers. Of course, she hadn't the funds to pay for the house yet, which was a predicament. Somehow, she needed to convince Lord Blackthorn to go along with her plan and give her the house.

"What are you concocting in that mind of yours?" Kate asked.

"Nothing," Amelia said, sipping coffee from her porcelain cup.

"I can always tell when you have something brewing in that head of yours." Kate gave her a sideward glance. "You are thinking of that delicious-looking man from last night, aren't you?"

When the butler entered the breakfast room, Amelia was relieved the attention was no longer on her. Both women turned to look at the man standing there like a statue, holding a silver tray. He said, "Miss Knight, this came for you."

Amelia thanked him and quickly broke the seal. She pulled the card out. When she saw the embossed name on the card, *Lord Richard Nickolas Blackthorn, the 9th Earl Blackthorn*, an icy chill ran up and down her spine, along with a feeling of horror.

"What does it say?"

She looked up from the notecard, her heart pounding wildly in her chest. "Lord Blackthorn requests that I come and retrieve my reticule I left behind in the carriage last night."

"Oh?" Kate looked confused, then wide-eyed, as she said, "That was the Earl Blackthorn?"

"Yes."

Kate snatched the notecard. "You've got to be jesting," she said, reading the note.

The man in the alley last night couldn't be Lord Blackthorn. Could he? Damn, he must have found her calling card in her reticule. She had made the mistake of bringing her pouch and then leaving it in her haste to get away from him, not to mention allowing him to drive her home. But then again, her own carriage was missing—had been stolen, rather.

She let out a doleful sigh. Surely he would never accept her proposal, knowing what she did. He must think she belonged in Bedlam. He would never take her offer seriously now.

"What will you do?" Kate asked, sipping her hot chocolate.

Move on to the next candidate? That would be better than facing Lord Blackthorn. By and by, how would she explain last night? She sighed heavily. "I don't know what I will do . . . yet."

"This is a perfect opportunity for you to speak to him about your proposal."

"Perhaps."

"But . . ."

What if the earl probed her about her past, her reasons for being at East End? One thing was certain, he could not know of her past. If he discovered she was the daughter of a whore, he would never take her offer seriously, and might even try to take advantage of her circumstances. She could never risk that.

Kate must have felt her reluctance. "We can discern that he is honorable and is willing to risk his life to assist us. That says something about his character, doesn't it?"

"It does," she agreed. "Hopefully, it won't be difficult to convince him."

She watched Kate's expression. Her late husband had been a very successful merchant and now she had all his fortune to do with as she wished. How fortunate of her to have the freedom that Amelia wanted so dearly.

"But then again, he can refuse." She looked at Kate and tried to smile. Oh, how much she needed Kate's spirit now with the recent discovery that the man who had heroically rescued her was the very man she would need to convince to join in on her risky plan.

Amelia recalled the first time she had met Kate. Her friend had had the audacity to excuse herself after dinner during a card game with the ladies, and had joined the men in their smoking room. She had noted there was no reason for the women to wait for the men to join them while they sat prettily like dolls. Amelia had instantly liked her, and they had been good friends since. Everyone tolerated Kate, according to Amelia's grandmamma, because she was a wealthy widow from Boston.

"Or he could say, 'Yes.'"

Surely, what would he think of her when she presented her proposal to him, knowing she was a woman who lurked about St. Giles in the middle of the night, with a pistol no less?

Oh, how she dreaded this meeting. She had one Season. One. If she wasn't careful, she would end up chattel of another man, and she refused to think on that horrid thought. She'd been a prisoner in her grandmother's house, and she would never be handed over to another man like property.

"What if he demands money now?" Amelia said out loud. As it was, if not for Kate's generosity, she would have a difficult time since Mrs. Pots managed her funds for the Season.

"Tell him the truth, that the money will not be available until after the wedding."

Amelia nodded. She didn't like extortion or threats, but if she had to, she would use the information she had gained about the late Lord Blackthorn's debt that now sat on the current earl's shoulders to persuade him.

Thoughts of last night paraded through her mind. "You are right, Kate. He didn't have to assist us last night, but he did, and that tells me that he is a man of honor, someone who is willing to put the safety of others before his own. I just have to convince him that he is helping a cause we will both benefit from in the end."

"Well said." Kate nodded.

Now if she could stop her heart from racing, it would help greatly. The truth was, she had no lineage, and she was certainly no lady. The only reason the *ton*, and Lord Blackthorn, would entertain her was because she would inherit her grandmother's wealth. And the English loved that prospect, didn't they? How could such a man take her seriously if he discovered the truth about where she came from?

Amelia thought about the last decade in Scotland with a heavy sigh. She had been in love once, but that short span of happiness had turned into an utter nightmare. If nothing else, her grandmother was right about one thing: Emotions only complicated matters and distorted one's judgment.

With the clank of cup and saucer, Amelia's thoughts shattered.

Kate looked at her, concern etched on her face. "Are you all right?"

Clearing her throat, Amelia said, "Yes . . . yes, of course." She had never told Kate about that night. She would rather forget it ever happened. When Amelia's gaze met Kate's, there were several seconds of weighty silence.

"Do you want me to go with you?"

She shook her head and smiled, pushing the memories back where she had kept them for nearly five years. "I'll be fine. Besides, who will divert Mrs. Pots if she looks for me?"

Her friend didn't smile as she'd hoped. "Don't be too long, that old woman will get suspicious before long."

"I will, and thank you," Amelia said, reaching out to pat her friend's hand. "You're a dear friend."

"I am dreadfully jealous, though, if you ask me," she said, her voice taking on a light, airy tone. "I hear the earl is a war hero." Kate smiled widely. "I love the ruggedly handsome war hero type."

"And rude." Amelia frowned. Even their tête-à-tête hadn't helped in the least, as her nerves were getting the best of her at the thought of seeing him again.

Chapter 7

AMELIA LOOKED UP at the neoclassical facade with recessed sash windows on the second floor. Above the door was a circular balcony with bright flowers woven in and out of the ironwork, and vines hanging loose from a flower pot.

She took a deep breath, placing one hand over her belly to ease the knot that tightened as each second ticked by. She inhaled deeply and knocked three times. For several seconds, there was no answer.

Looking at the card she held in her hand, she checked the address again. *What must be keeping him?*

She looked around the street and noticed passersby, so she pulled her bonnet down to hide her face. Another tight knot twisted in her stomach, her nerves increasing by the second. She had taken every precaution to get here, including sneaking out of the house donning a simple dress and a plain bonnet. On a positive note, the house was only three blocks from her rented townhouse, so she'd be able to return home in time.

Why was she so nervous? She was here to thank the man and retrieve her reticule. That was all. But in truth, he held the key to her freedom. She needed him to agree to partake in her plan, so she had to make sure he could not refuse her. English aristocracy loved money, so much so that they overlooked most offenses.

After breakfast, she had rehearsed what she would say to Lord Blackthorn. She had recited the words so many times she gave herself a headache. Touching her chest, as if that would slow her heart, she used the silver door knocker to alert the house again.

Still no answer.

She looked at the card. This *was* the correct address. She had only an hour at most until Mrs. Pots returned from Grafton House on Bond Street where she was off posting Amelia's letter to her grandmother. The woman had informed her she was not her personal servant. Still, in the end, she'd had no choice but to abide by Amelia's wishes, once she'd informed her chaperone that the missive contained information her grandma was waiting for.

The butler finally opened the door. "May I help you, miss?"

Amelia handed him the card.

"Ah, yes. Please come in, miss."

She stepped into the white marble foyer of the impeccably fashioned townhouse with an open staircase with a dark wood balustrade. There was a light floral scent that was quite inviting, and soft pink peonies in elongated vases throughout. Quite feminine, which begged the question, whose house was this?

"This way," the butler said, and gestured for her to follow him. She had a dreadful thought that perhaps Lord Blackthorn may already have a wife and her grandmother had been wrong about him.

Amelia twirled her thumbs together, a nervous habit, as she followed the butler down the hall. Somehow, each step felt heavier than the last, as if her feet sank deep in a muddy pit. *Stop being so nervous.* But the thought of him refusing her made her nauseous and, after last night and assessing his temperamental disposition, it was a good possibility that he might tell her exactly what he thought of her proposal and send her on her way.

The butler stopped in front of a double door, knocked once, and opened it to introduce her to the two people in the parlor before leaving.

Lord Blackthorn saw her and stood ceremoniously. His handsome smile ceased as his gaze met hers.

Her stomach dropped at his grimace. In fact, he seemed downright irritated to see her. This would prove very difficult, she was certain of it. Her mind ordered her to enter the room, but her feet felt bolted to the floor.

The woman next to Lord Blackthorn observed her. There was nothing English about her. Her black hair was in a bun with loose curls hanging down her neck, and dark golden skin brought out her unusual eyes. They were curious and sharp.

Was she his wife? Disappointment pulsed through Amelia again. Her grandmother had assured her that the men on the list were bachelors. It wasn't like her to make a mistake. But then again, it could have been a short engagement if she was with child. The exotic woman gazed at Lord Blackthorn, then at Amelia. Amelia was certain the woman's life wasn't lacking male company, and it clearly did not exclude Lord Blackthorn. The thought made her feel quite nettled.

"You must be Miss Knight. I'm Zara. Please, come in," she said.

Blackthorn watched Amelia. He had a quiet strength about him now, like that of a warrior ready to thunder down on his enemy at a moment's notice. Her gaze dropped to his impeccably tailored cravat, then to his tailcoat and tight breeches before swooping up again to the breadth of his broad shoulders. Eyeing the solid column of his neck, she lifted her gaze to meet his green eyes that reminded her of a dewy forest just before sunrise. She dropped her gaze and looked at his dark fitted breeches and the well-formed mound between his legs.

Even *she*, a woman who never intended to be seduced, could not deny the physical attraction she felt for him. Suddenly, her clothes felt a little too tight and the air in the room a little too stifling.

"Are you all right?" Zara said.

Amelia looked at the woman next to him. Lord Blackthorn's mouth pulled into a thin line at the woman's question. Before Amelia could answer, Zara said, "Why don't I leave you two to discuss . . ." The woman watched Lord Blackthorn, then Amelia, before finishing her sentence. ". . . whatever it is you both need to discuss. Fetch me when you are finished here, darling. You know where I will be."

Darling? So, they were intimate. *Why is that not a surprise?* Amelia thought with disappointment.

Once the woman left the parlor, Lord Blackthorn gestured for Amelia to sit. Amelia stepped into the parlor but didn't go too far into the space. "Thank you, but I prefer to stand."

"Suit yourself," he said, and walked over to the hearth and leaned against it, still looking at her.

Neither of them said a word for several seconds.

"Is something wrong?" she finally said, breaking the silence.

"Of course not," he said. "Why do you ask?"

"You're staring at me rather strangely." She should approach him with her proposal now, but she needed to calm her nerves; otherwise, she would no doubt botch up the proposal.

He ran his fingers through his hair. "It's not you. I must confess, I didn't get much sleep last night."

"On that note, I want to thank you again. Your assistance was most welcomed."

The expression on his face made her want to take it back. Last night had been traumatic enough on everyone. No matter what the reasons were for his foul disposition, she vowed to not take it personally.

"If I gave you any sign that I wasn't grateful, I do apologize." She tried to keep her tone even, but those piercing green eyes were rather unnerving, and she wished he would stop looking at her as if she were a bug to be crushed.

She waited for him to acknowledge her comment, but he didn't.

"The reticule?"

"Of course," he said. Walking to the console, he retrieved her small silk reticule and handed it to her. "Here is it, Miss Knight."

"Thank you, Lord Blackthorn." A botched introduction was all she needed. This entire situation was one disaster after another.

Time ticked awkwardly for several more seconds. How to even start the conversation? She hated feeling this way, this uncertainty that gripped her. Damn, he looked even more irritated. Clearing her throat, she regained her courage and told herself to stop acting like a damn schoolgirl. "Please tell your wife I—"

"Wife?"

"Yes," she said. "Isn't Miss Zara your wife?" *His wife. Who else could she be*, Amelia thought, defeat pulsing through her.

His brows lifted. "The last time I checked, I was quite single."

She let out a sigh of relief. She had never thought one sterile, single word could bring such relief. Then it quickly dawned on her *who* the woman really was. His mistress. So, he was no different after all. Why did this surprise her again?

The exotic beauty was a highly paid...

She hated to think of the word. Her mother had been a whore and her grandmother made sure she knew exactly what her mother had been doing with those men. Hot resentment bubbled in her chest when memories of her mother flashed into her mind's eye. She had refused to believe it at first, but she had seen these men with her own eyes.

Amelia bit back the resentment she had kept at bay for so many years. *My son had indulged, and he was weak and emotional. Look what it got him. Dead,* her grandmother had said to her years ago. *If you are to survive in this world, you must learn to rise above these useless, base needs that have no place in survival.*

Her mother had never talked of her father. Every time she had asked about him, her mother had teared up and ignored her questions. To her grandmother, marrying for title, position, and pedigree was survival. The old woman wanted no less from Amelia for giving her a home. If she didn't deliver, her grandmother would strip her of everything.

The mistress was none of her concern. Still, the thought of them together made her hot with mixed feelings she couldn't name. "Oh, I see . . ."

"Is something troubling you?" Lord Blackthorn asked.

"Of course not. What you do here is your business, not mine."

He looked confused for a second, then understanding seemed to dawn on him. "You're right, it's none of your business why I am here, but this isn't a brothel."

"If you insist."

He took several steps toward her, now standing only a few feet away. For a moment, he looked as though he might give her another spiteful retort. She held her breath for the blow, waiting. Then, slowly, his gaze lowered to her lips, and remained there. His eyes blazed with sudden desire. Oh, heavens, he looked as though he might kiss her. Yes, yes, yes.

No, no, no. What was she thinking? In the midst of her own ridiculous fray, she heard him speak.

"Is there anything else you wish to discuss before we conclude our business? Or would you like to insult Zara some more?"

"It wasn't my intension to insult anyone. I was merely here to retrieve my pouch per your instructions and to thank you for your help."

He frowned, his brows pulling together tightly. "You have a hell of a way of showing your gratitude."

"I can see coming here was a mistake," she said, lifting her chin.

"I will agree with you fully in that regard."

"I will be on my way then."

"Good."

Christ, the stubborn, reckless, and self-righteous woman had the gall to come in here and insult everyone. He hated the way his body had betrayed him when she entered the parlor. She was beautiful, there was no denying that, and she very well knew it. Annoyingly so, and he was certain those damn curves, that flawless skin, and those full lips beckoned every breathing gentleman in London to abide by her wishes. Well, he was not one of them.

Damn, what was it about her that troubled him? He hardly knew the woman. It was not as if he'd never seen an attractive woman before. She was an heiress who had the gall to conduct herself as she pleased. Perhaps he was lacking a woman's company. *That must be it.*

He ran his hand through the thick of his hair and down his face with equal parts frustration and fatigue. He had this sudden urge to plant a facer. Perhaps a boxing match would get the energy out of his system. Yes, that sounded good just about now. Perhaps he'd call on Gentleman Jackson on Bond Street, or in an alleyway. Either would do just fine at this moment.

"Has your lovely girl gone?" Zara said as she entered the parlor.

He didn't face her. "She isn't mine, far from it."

She walked over to him and linked her warm fingers though his, just as she had done many times long ago. "Care for some distraction, my darling?"

He pulled his hands away from her. Walking over to the window, he faced the busy street.

"What is the matter?" she said, coming to stand next to him.

He looked at her. "What makes you think there is anything wrong?"

"My darling, I've known you a long time . . ." She paused. "Is this about Miss Knight?"

"No."

"I think it is," she said. "I have never seen you so affected by a woman before. Not even me, as I recall."

He didn't want to have this conversation. As it was, he needed to head back to his townhouse to make certain his mother had removed all her things to Blackthorn Hall.

She ignored his question. "Miss Knight," she went on. "You never mentioned how you came to know her."

"An unfortunate encounter."

She watched him. "Curious response," she said. "I hear she's worth a fortune, and she's here to find a husband. Am I to surmise you are not one of the men who are fighting for her affection?"

"If I am considering marriage, which I am not, she is the last person on Earth I would want as a wife."

Zara's eyes narrowed. "Now I know you are lying."

Blackthorn gave her a peck on the forehead. It wasn't that he didn't find Zara attractive. She was a beautiful and brave woman who had made something of herself when she escaped the slums with her cunning. This tactic of hers would have worked on him months ago, but now, it had lost its potency. He was tired, and all he wanted was to get the hell out of London as soon as his business with Kendall was dealt with. The only reason he had come to London in the past was to see his brother, Max. Now, with him gone, there was nothing here for Blackthorn.

She observed him for a while and she finally said, "I know the look of a man who's besotted."

By the time Amelia reached her townhouse, she was irked—no, she was more than irked. So much so that she almost slammed the front door, and she had never done that, not since she was thirteen.

When she was young, this resentment and anger would

have turned into tears she'd shed when she was alone. Until Mrs. Pots came to fetch her for another lesson and a fitting for another ridiculous, overpriced dress.

This unsettling emotion was like an unyielding storm that was wreaking havoc on her life. She didn't know how to manage this . . . this unsettling feeling of disappointment. Why was she allowing this man to affect her this way? Just because he was no longer a choice, it didn't mean an end to her plan. She'd simply have to move on to the next man on the list.

The thought didn't ease her mind. Not in the least.

Kate had once said Amelia would have to face her demons. Amelia hadn't asked her to elaborate. Despite their friendship, she never spoke to Kate about her parents. It was too painful, and almost made her weep and left her confused in the end.

She bit her lip and closed her eyes. Lord Blackthorn seemed to bring out the worst in her. Perhaps it was better that she'd realized just how unsuitable he was for her plan.

She walked up the stairs and made her way to her room before Mrs. Pots returned from her errands. Pulling her bonnet off, she tossed it on the chair next to the fireplace. Moments later, Kate opened the door and quietly slipped into her room.

"Well? How did it go?"

She plopped down on the chair by the fireplace, quite unladylike, and realized she had demolished the pretty bonnet. Fiddling with it, she said, "Not well."

"What do you mean, exactly?" Kate said, sitting on the edge of Amelia's bed.

"We had a disagreement."

"I see."

Amelia looked at her friend and sighed heavily. "It's impossible trying to talk to that man. He is so arrogant, egotistical, and—"

"Rude," Kate added with a faint smile.

"Yes," she affirmed. "He is, very much so." She rubbed the back of her neck to release the tightness there. "It doesn't matter now. I will have to move on to the next candidate."

"So, he refused your proposal?"

"Not exactly," she said. "All right, I didn't have the chance to bring it up."

"Because he is . . . rude?" Kate said again with a faint smirk.

Amelia gave her a sideward glance. "It's not just that. There is something about him that brings out the worst in me. I am certain he will not agree to my proposal."

"You don't know that until you speak with him first," Kate said. "You will simply have to convince him. I am sure he can appreciate that."

"The man is so intolerable." Even while she was saying these words, she knew Kate was right. There was a reason she had asked Kate to come with her to London. Amelia had been too sheltered, and she needed a friend who could make her see the possibilities.

"You didn't think this was going to be easy, did you?" Kate said with an encouraging smile. "You want to be sure he isn't interested before you move on to the next man on the list. After all, there are only three options."

"Perhaps I can write to him and propose my plan that

way." That sounded more appealing than having to face the ill-tempered man.

"You can," she said. "But will you be satisfied with that?"

Amelia wasn't certain. Secretly, she hoped Lord Blackthorn would not present himself at the ball tonight. Surely the inheritance would convince him. What man in his right mind would say no to that kind of sum? "I will think on the matter," she said. "You will be there, won't you?"

"I'd love to go with you, but I have this matter I must remedy."

"Is everything all right?"

"Yes and no," Kate said. "It's about my late husband."

Kate had mentioned her late husband had passed in Boston five years ago, but that was all she had said on that matter. "Is it serious?" Amelia asked.

"No, just some things I need to go over with my lawyer. He is in town. Go to the ball and have a good time. There is the verb conjugation on your desk. Mrs. Pots left it for you before she went to mail your letter to your grandmother."

Amelia rolled her eyes in defiance. She was the last person on Earth still conjugating verbs at twenty. But that wasn't what was making her nervous. Proposing her idea to him made her stomach churn, and if she could avoid it, she would.

She picked up the parchment with the list of names. All right, Lord Blackthorn, let's see what you have to say . . .

Chapter 8

Lord Grayson's Ball
London

AMELIA ENTERED LORD Grayson's grand ballroom
with Mrs. Pots by her side. The butler announced her
name, the sound punching the air like glass shattering.
Heads turned, and her stomach knotted. She felt like a tiny
specimen to be gawked at and prodded. The members of the
ton's gazes were full of curiosity. A few smiled, while several
chaperones donned a look of distaste in their shrewd eyes
as if to say, *competition.*

Given that this was her first formal introduction to the
ton, she told herself it was only protocol. Still, she gulped.
The scene before her was nothing short of extravagance, as
were the guests. She felt unnerved and out of place, even
though she'd been trained for this day. A decade of training,
to be exact.

"Well," Mrs. Pots said, nudging her with her elbow. The
woman's plainly coiffured hair and her drab gown stood out
like an eyesore. "Go fetch a husband."

Amelia fought a frown. "I just arrived."

"All three of the men on the list are here."

"How do you know this?"

"I have my ways," she said. "You're here for one reason—to find a husband—and I am here to make certain you do exactly that."

Even before her chaperone finished the sentence, Amelia was searching for *him*. She told herself that it was only to make sure she didn't humiliate herself in front of him again. *Better yet, forget the exchange you had with the earl this morning*, she told herself as she walked deep into the ballroom with her chaperone. *Pretend it didn't happen*. It was the only way she could move forward. Several gentlemen looked her way and smiled. Then another. And another.

"Don't flatter yourself. It's your inheritance they want," Mrs. Pots whispered to her.

Amelia couldn't understand why the woman held such a grudge against her. As it was, she didn't feel purposeful or brave tonight. In fact, if she had her way, she wouldn't be here at all. This was purely a means to an end, she reminded herself, and she wanted it to be over as quickly as possible.

She took a deep breath, her palm on her stomach, and tried to ease the tension mounting in her neck and shoulders. Mrs. Pots gripped her arm and Amelia jerked, her heart wildly thumping in her chest.

"What is wrong with you tonight?" Mrs. Pots said. "Get in there."

"Do not rush me," Amelia hissed. "The prospect of choosing a husband without a proper courtship, or any regard for my opinion, isn't something every girl dreams about."

The woman observed her carefully with those familiar calculating eyes Amelia detested so much. "Go and take your pick. I don't wish to be here any longer than we need to."

"I don't need you to remind me," Amelia said, annoyed.

The woman glared at her. "I don't understand you. Most women don't have a choice in the matter, but your grandmother gave you a choice, although I cannot fathom why. I suggest you be grateful." She paused as if concocting what she wanted to say next. "Go, get in there. I will get us refreshments." She walked away before Amelia could respond, ignoring Society's protocol that she remain by Amelia's side.

Normally, Amelia couldn't have cared less what she did now. But in this room, in front of these people, she couldn't afford gossip. Amelia watched Mrs. Pots disappear among the crowd. She stood alone in the grand ballroom with all these guests, exposed.

When Mrs. Pots had returned from her errand this morning, there had been something odd about her. She'd been reserved, deep in her thoughts. What was her chaperone concocting in her head?

Had she discovered Amelia had sneaked out of the house last night? Or discovered her plan to annul the marriage?

The woman had even canceled the afternoon tea and reading of the Bible. It would be a disastrous end if she'd somehow discovered Amelia had no intention of staying married to anyone.

Breathing in deeply once more, she took in the scenery and the grandeur of the ballroom. A sparkle of shimmering lights reflected off the crystal glass of the chandeliers, and the scent of flowers lingered in the air as impeccably dressed footmen walked around catering to the guests. This magical night seemed to promise a fairytale to come. Even she could not deny the sense of freedom and excitement she felt just now. And the ivory silk dress her modiste had sewn together with exquisite detail made her feel, dare she think it, magical.

Although she had not been allowed to attend every event growing up in Scotland, her grandmother's annual ball was extravagant, and a treat. She'd sit back in the farthest level of the stairs, watch the guests, and dream of the day she would be free of the place. Meanwhile, she had been schooled in all aspects of good breeding. When she was finally allowed to attend the ball at the age of seventeen, she had learned to play the part her grandmother had wanted her to play: a properly educated, well-bred lady.

Yet tonight, being here, her senses were heightened, and she felt terribly clumsy.

The ball was in full motion, and Blackthorn heard the familiar music before he entered the grand ballroom on the ground floor. The fragrant aromas of beeswax and flowers permeated the hallway as he approached the ballroom. Hundreds of candles adorned the sconces and reflected from the chandeliers. The servants gracefully walked about the room in their liveries, serving guests their drinks.

He forced a grin and slowly walked into the ballroom.

The crowd hushed in waves, then came to a painful silence. All eyes were on him instantly, and he felt a need to get the hell out of there. He didn't like this. Despite being the son of an earl, he had never felt at home in this place. Among these guests, he could not deny the emptiness. He looked around, scanning the room for familiar faces.

Lately he had wanted, needed to share what he had seen—death, war, and destruction. But with whom? It was always a faceless someone. He'd been feeling this way since his brother passed, not quite understanding why. He told himself this was what happened when one had faced death in war and spent years around the world spying for king and country. A part of him was hollowed, empty, and nothing in this world would fill that void. He accepted this reality as he had accepted all the missions without hesitation.

He chuckled inwardly. He was skilled at pretending he was someone else, going from mission to mission. But he wasn't playing a part now. He *was* the new Lord Blackthorn. Here, he couldn't hide. Here, he was confined to the rules set forth by his forefathers, rules that would define him and eventually suck the life out of him. Fortunately, he wouldn't be staying long.

He yanked at his tight cravat, which suddenly felt all too confining. What he needed was a tall drink. Or two.

He scanned the room, but what or who he was searching for, he wasn't sure. One nameless beauty after another. Young and naïve. There must be nearly three hundred people here tonight. Scanning the crowd for a friendly face, he found none. Chatham was on his honeymoon with his new bride, and most of his brother spies for the Home Secretary were out of the county by the orders of the Prince Regent.

The blond woman caught his attention. Her figure was regal, with curves that tickled his fingers. He inched closer. The woman reached back with her long, delicate fingers to touch the hook of the silver necklace donning her slender neck. Inching closer again, he kept his gaze on her. The thought of those hands wrapped around his manhood, stroking the crown, made him tight with need. She turned her head to look at the gentleman next to her and something akin to jealousy ensued.

Then familiarity . . .

Amelia Knight. Damn the bloody woman.

He stopped dead in his tracks as his mind grappled with the idea of her. His body wanted her, but his mind warned against that very idea. In truth, he didn't want to spend his entire evening quarreling, with her assaulting him every way possible. He had better things to do, like go off somewhere quiet and drink a bottle of scotch in peace.

Why was he even here?

Ah, yes. He'd promised Grayson he'd stop by.

Seeing well above the crowd, he searched for a drink. Even now, the crowd slowly dribbled into the ballroom from the hallway. As he walked toward the footman holding a silver tray, he saw Elizabeth Deveraux and his mother approaching him. He grimaced.

Too late to leave, as they had spotted him. He scowled and fisted his hands.

"There you are," his mother said, joining him.

"Ladies," he said. No doubt she had decided to conveniently forget their conversation in his study last night. His mother had a talent for selective memory. Otherwise, how did one go about the way she did without any recourse for her actions? Was the room getting more crowded? He looked around and noticed several groups of women and men feigning business, but he was keenly aware they were eavesdropping.

"It's been a long time, my lord. Too long," Elizabeth said, her tone light and sweet.

"I heard about your husband," he said in a solemn tone. Elizabeth's expression changed. Did he detect a hint of sadness in those shrewd eyes?

"Did you hear about the heiress?" she said quickly, avoiding his comment.

No matter how much Elizabeth would deny it, she loved gossip and those with the most fortune. In this case, he surmised she wanted to know if he was interested in the woman. Was she looking for a reaction from him?

"Which one?" Blackthorn said. His mother frowned. There were several women who each had over twenty thousand pounds in dower. You could usually tell by the size of the crowd around the young woman, if one were to really assess the situation, which he had no interest in doing.

"The heiress from Scotland. I was informed she would be attending tonight."

She was here all right, and she wanted Somersby Hall. *God knows why.* That house was a curse to the family, and he meant to rid himself of it quickly so that he could pay off the damn debt, close down the houses, and leave London.

"I'm sorry to disappoint you, ladies, but I must be off." After a few drinks to take the edge off, he intended to approach the heiress about her interest in Somersby Hall.

"Where are you going?" his mother said.

"Somewhere quiet."

"Oh, I see Philip," his mother said, giving no thought to what he'd just said. "I hear he recently returned from abroad. I must go speak with him. Come, Elizabeth."

Blackthorn gazed at the young man standing proudly at his father's side. Philip sipped his drink and smiled at the young woman he was conversing with. Some said Philip had inherited his late mother's principles. While Philip may stand for all that was moral, his father, Sir Kendall, was quite the opposite.

Blackthorn looked at his mother. "Do as you wish."

"I will. I just wish my only son would learn to enjoy what life has to offer," she said, and crossed the room with Elizabeth to greet Philip.

Blackthorn slowly unleashed his breath. Then, from the periphery, he felt someone approach. He sensed it before he knew. An unwelcome visitor. He made his attempt to quickly walk away. Too late.

"Ah, your mother is looking quite . . . well," Sir Kendall said with an amused tone.

This is going to be one hell of a night.

"And Lady Deveraux seems to have recovered from her husband's passing," Sir Kendall added, giving him a knowing look. There was a hint of insolence in Kendall's voice.

"If you say so."

"I didn't think you would show tonight," Kendall said.

"Why is that?"

"Let's just say you don't seem the sort to enjoy these types of gatherings."

The man was perceptive, which made Blackthorn wonder if he was spying on him. "If you'll excuse me." He started to walk away.

"Just a moment, young man."

Blackthorn stopped in his tracks. The thought of teaching Kendall some manners gave him a great deal of pleasure now. Normally, he wasn't one to let others dictate his behavior, and living the life of a spy had taught him to play the part well in that regard. But he detested bullies, especially ones that threatened him.

He turned around and glared at Kendall. "What?" he uttered, letting all formalities fall.

When Blackthorn had discovered his father owed an insurmountable sum, he had dug deeper and found out this bully owned a high-priced brothel and gaming halls. Oh, yes, he knew of the brothel and women, the so-called high-priced Cyprians that Kendall controlled with an iron fist. He catered to the highest bidders of the *ton*, but what Society was blind to was that the owner was not a woman Kendall had strategically placed in these brothels, but Kendall himself.

"I suggest you listen if you know what is good for you," Kendall hissed.

"Do not threaten me, old man," Blackthorn whispered. "I am aware of your dealings ... your so-called 'businesses.'"

Kendall's lips thinned and his eyes narrowed.

"You will not approach me again regarding this matter. I gave you my word you will get your damn money."

Shaking his head, Kendall noted, "Lucky your father is dead. He would surely be disappointed to see you treat his friends with such impudence. After what I did for him."

"You have a canny way of twisting the truth," Blackthorn murmured.

"If you knew the entire truth . . ." Kendall grinned.

"Do not mistake who you are addressing. Unlike my father, I choose not to skulk in the presence of a gutless bully."

Kendall's eyes widened, and his lips thinned like a tight string. "How dare you. I make it my business to make certain I come out the victor, so if I were you, I'd be a little more grateful that I didn't call in the debt today."

"Get out of my sight," Blackthorn warned.

"If I don't see the money in thirty days, you *will* regret it," Kendall warned. "I would hate to see your name appear in the headlines of *The London Times*, or better yet, see you die in a debtor's prison."

Cutting a glare, the pig walked away. Blackthorn raked his hand through his hair and took a deep breath to ease the mounting urge to beat the hell out of Kendall. He'd been in prison while on a mission, and he didn't give a damn about his name appearing in any gossip columns.

Walking in the opposite direction of Kendall, he saw Lord Benedict Grayson near the tall window across the room. Grayson, who wore a ridiculously wide grin on his face, was speaking with someone. It must be a woman—why else would he don such a ridiculous smile? But Blackthorn couldn't tell who at his angle, as a tall gentleman was blocking her. He inched closer to greet his friend and take his mind off the unpleasant encounter with Kendall.

As he approached, Grayson was drooling all over the mystery—

Oh, hell. *Amelia Knight*, he said to himself when the gentleman blocking his view of her walked off with the woman he was speaking with.

Her hair was pulled up in a loose bun and secured with an ornate pin, showcasing her silky neck, one that was meant to be kissed. Even now, his fingers itched to loosen her hair and let it tumble down like a waterfall, but another part of him wanted to turn on his heel and walk away.

Grayson gently cupped her elbow and leaned in a little, whispering something in her ear. A twinge of envy pricked Blackthorn. Grayson saw him approach and threw him a look that said *hands off—I saw her first*. Simply to vex him, if nothing else. They'd always had a healthy dose of rivalry. Blackthorn's gaze moved down the curves of her body, and again his body reacted without his permission.

Miss Knight, the heiress who'd had the audacity to walk out after a heated argument. He saw her smile and his mouth pulled into a grin. *You're an idiotic fool*. His gaze lowered to her chest, the perfect bosom that rose and fell. Her hand moved up to fiddle with the stone on the necklace. He continued to approach.

"Blackthorn," Grayson said, "I'd like to introduce Miss Amelia Knight."

Blackthorn cocked his brow, waiting to see what she would say.

"We've met," she said with a polite smile.

Grayson looked rather amused. "I see," he said. "Well, then . . ." He observed them both. "I guess there is no need for introductions."

"I apologize," Miss Knight said, "but I am in need of refreshment."

"Of course. Shall we?" Grayson said with a wide grin.

"Might I have a word, Miss Knight?" Blackthorn instinctively reached out and nearly grabbed her elbow, but stopped when the group of women took notice.

She looked back at him. "Oh?" She looked at Lord Grayson's questioning gaze.

"If the lady wishes it, Blackthorn."

Amelia looked at Grayson and smiled before turning back to Blackthorn. "I'm rather . . . parched, my lord. Perhaps another time. If you will excuse me." She proceeded to allow Grayson to guide her to the refreshments table.

He watched her walk off with Grayson with disappointment squeezing his chest. Not quite understanding this strange feeling, he turned and walked off in the opposite direction. Parched? What kind of damn excuse was that?

Bloody woman.

Amelia pulled her cloak tightly around her to ward off the chill outside the ballroom. She liked the cool breeze on her warm face. She had been feeling suffocated in there. Lord

Grayson seemed to be an amiable man. She enjoyed his company and kindness. Perhaps he would take part in her plans, instead of Lord Blackthorn. The idea was enticing, but something in her didn't entirely agree with the idea.

Looking up, she saw a few stars dotted between the scattered clouds. The moon peeked through the clouds brightly. She smiled. The distant music slowly faded, and silence engulfed her as she walked farther away from the entrance of the ballroom. From where she stood, she could see the dazzling lights through the tall windows, guests drinking and enjoying themselves. She had to admit, even with her distaste for this type of gathering, she somehow felt enchanted by it all for once. But, in the end, she had never felt she belonged here, and in truth she didn't.

Looking back, she noticed someone exit the ball, and she continued on a narrow pathway toward the manicured rose garden. Ahead of her, there was a private area with a bench surrounded by trees.

Having no wish to converse with anyone, especially Lord Blackthorn, she walked ahead to the trees where she hoped to ensconce herself. Once there, she sat down on the bench and hoped the trees would shield her from prying eyes.

When she heard footfalls coming toward her, she held her breath. Suddenly, she was all too aware of her response to being watched. *You're being ridiculous. No one is staring at you.*

When all was quiet, she let out her breath. It must be the stress and the pressure of having to choose a husband she didn't want. These people. This place. At times, the thought of playing the part her grandmother wished was almost too much to bear. But memories of her childhood helped to refuel her resolve and remind her where she came from: the slums, born to a fallen woman who had given her only child away.

But this place brought back too many memories and too much shame. These people who had once viewed Amelia as a thing in the streets, called her filth and poor, now gathered around her with compliments.

Cook had been kind, and he truly cared for *her*. Not like these vultures circling around her because of her inheritance. Perhaps, when all this was over, she would look for him. She wanted nothing to do with these people, yet she needed them. How conflicting was that?

The image of Lord Blackthorn rescuing her like a gallant knight came to her—not that she knew what a gallant knight would look like. But she knew the reality. He wasn't what she pictured; no, he was a highborn privileged lord, just like the rest she had come to know. Still, he had helped her and Kate in the alley the other day. Maybe he couldn't live with himself had he turned a blind eye to their desperate need, so there must be some good in him.

She heard footfalls coming closer.

Then closer again.

Then came a very familiar voice. "You shouldn't be out here alone."

She stood up from the bench and stepped closer to the trunk of the nearest tree, as if it should shield her. "You startled me," she blurted out. The hood of her cloak fell back as she looked up at his gaze. Under the moon, the distinct contours of his face cast a shadow that made him look aloof, dark, and foreboding. He reminded her of a dark knight ready to do battle at a moment's notice. His gaze didn't miss a beat as it lowered to her lips . . . her neck, and down to her bosom. She pulled her cloak closed and held it tight.

The breeze tousled his hair, and his expression softened, becoming almost gentle. She wondered what he looked like when he smiled. And why must he look quite so irritatingly handsome? Under his gaze, she felt exposed and discomfited.

Clearing her throat, she said, "I . . . I must be heading back. I am certain Mrs. Pots will be looking for me by now." She walked several steps but halted at the sound of his voice. Her heart pumped harder and faster as each second ticked by.

"Wait," he said. He looked as though he were contemplating something. "Take a walk with me?"

Walk with him? Alone, in the dark? The thought made her heart leap with uncertainty. Why would he possibly want this? He had made it clear to her exactly what he thought about her, hadn't he? "Why?" she blurted out. There was no point in ceremony with this man. They'd passed that.

He regarded her for several seconds. "A curious response."

"It's a perfectly natural response."

"If you say so," he replied smoothly.

"Why do you persist in seeking me out? You made your intention clear to me."

He took several steps forward and stopped. "I see you are still harboring ill will from this morning."

"I am most certainly not," she said. "Besides, you don't know me well enough to make that judgement."

"Of course you are," he said. "I make it my business to know people. Rest assured, Miss Knight, seeking you out was the last thing I wanted to do tonight, but it's important I speak with you."

Ugh. So he wanted something from her, just like every other gentleman in this blasted town. Already she had the attention of several gentlemen and Lord Grayson because of her inheritance. They were like a pack of wolves closing in on their prize. Why else would he seek her out? "Very well, say what you must."

"I rather hoped we could do this in private."

"There is no one here," she said, looking about.

"I beg to differ." His eyes guided her to look far left beyond the garden.

Shaking her head, she said, "I don't see anyone." Certainly, the man was observant. This made her wonder what else he had been spying on. She must really be cautious with him.

"I insist."

She narrowed her eyes at him, trying to discern what exactly he wanted from her. "Very well, but I'd like to get this over with as quickly as possible." As silly as it was, she felt so unsure of herself when she was around him.

"Give me a few minutes head start. Follow me into the ballroom. Turn left. Down the hall, another left. It's the third door to your left. Knock twice."

She nodded, pulled her hood over her head, and watched him leave.

Blackthorn entered the house and walked toward the library. With each step away from her, thoughts of Miss Knight became solid in his mind. She may indeed be reckless and stubborn, but he was beginning to admire her courage.

As soon as he entered the library, he saw Elizabeth by the hearth. Immediately, she looked at him, her expression dour, almost sad. He left the door ajar and strolled in, but only far enough to keep a discreet distance.

"I didn't realize anyone was in here." He didn't trust her one bit. After returning home from the war, he'd discovered she had married an earl. Their promise had meant nothing to her. There had been no letter, no apology. Her entire dismissal of their relationship had been enough to show him just how cowardly she really was. But then again, he'd been too young to comprehend the gravity of his commitment.

"I had hoped to see you here," she said, lowering her gaze. She bit her lower lip as she used to do when she wasn't certain how to approach him. He could never deny her then, but it was different now. "As I recall, libraries were your favorite place to escape."

He didn't want to encourage her behavior. In truth, there was nothing between them, not even if he tried to salvage what they'd once had so long ago. "I must go."

"Wait. Stay."

"I really can't."

"Will you not allow me the courtesy to explain, Richard?"

"Courtesy?" he started. "Interesting choice of words."

"Oh, my darling, I had no choice, you see . . ." She paused, as if she were struggling to speak. "Papa threatened—"

"You owe me no explanation, my lady. Not anymore."

"Richard," she said, reaching for him, and he stepped back. "Please, will you give me a chance to explain, after all we've been through?"

He didn't allow himself to think on this. She was manipulative, and her words akin to poison. "This is highly inappropriate."

"Even after all we've been through?"

A few kisses here and there, and promises she'd broken. "You made your choice. *You* must live with it."

She paused and looked squarely at him, watching him as if calculating her next move. "All right. I don't know what I can do to change your opinion of me." She paused and took a step closer to him. "But know this. If there is any hope that you may find it in your heart to forgive me, I will endeavor to make that happen."

Not in your lifetime, he thought. There was a time he would have believed her, but now her words felt like shards of broken glass under his bare feet. He had been a damn idiotic fool to not see her true self; but then again, they had been too young.

A knock at the door broke the silence. *Bloody hell.* The damn door opened wider, and the angelic beauty stood before him, her smile fading . . .

"Miss Knight," Lord Blackthorn said. "The countess was just leaving." He gestured for her to leave.

The two women observed each other most curiously.

Then the countess turned to him with a sensual smile. "Until next time, *my* lord."

Amelia watched as the countess leaned in toward her to whisper in her ear.

"He's in a feisty mood tonight. Please do take caution with him."

Honestly, everywhere she looked, women were either ogling him with girlish whispers or seeking him out with no shame in the hope of gaining his attention.

As the door clicked shut, Lord Blackthorn said, "The countess was—"

"How you conduct yourself with the countess in private is of no concern to me." She stepped deep into the study with an undeniable disappointment pinching her heart.

He observed her as if she were an oddity he could not discern. Disappointment slowly seeped deeper into her veins. What did she expect from this man? For him to be a handsome knight in shining armor come to rescue her? Why was she letting herself feel this way?

"Are you always this blunt?" he said, breaking the silence.

She watched as he walked to her. Her initial reaction was to take a step back, but she didn't move for fear that he may see right through her. It seemed for a moment he had something to say, so she waited, but all he did was run his hands through the thick of his hair as if frustrated. Troubled, even. She looked at him. Really looked at him, and for a moment, she thought she saw a flicker of grief lingering in his eyes.

That instant, she realized she had never cared to consider if this man might have troubles of his own. What could a titled man with everything he could ever want in this world be concerned about? All the women of the *ton* flocked to him as if he were the last man in London, and he had the kind of freedom she desired—to live out his life as he pleased.

"Are you always this arrogant?" she said, when what she wanted was to know what was troubling him. The man brought out the worst in her, she thought.

He said nothing for a moment.

From the proximity of him, his lingering fragrance was too enticing and made her feel strange and nervous. Her heart leaped quicker at the thought of the changed disposition between them. All he was doing was standing there looking at her and she felt so exposed. Her gaze lowered and took in the entirety of him. He was dressed in his impeccably fitted suit that made her feel strangely warm. His mustard-yellow waistcoat framed by a dark blue tailcoat fit his broad chest perfectly. His cream breeches showcased his fine legs to perfection. Everything about him was flawless. Too perfect.

He carefully watched her as if he were trying to read her thoughts. Beyond the facade, there was something else there, something she could not name, and the way he was looking at her made her very uneasy. "What did you want to speak to me about?" she said.

He sighed heavily. "Why don't we start with a proper introduction . . . to start anew? Yes?"

She nodded.

He took her hand and placed it in his as if she were a fragile doll. His hand was warm and surprisingly calloused. This was not the hand of a man who lived a luxurious and privileged lifestyle. He lowered his lips and kissed her knuckles, sending tingles up and down her arm.

"It's a pleasure to meet you again, Miss Knight."

Her instinct told her to pull her hand away, but she couldn't. Didn't. Instead, she wanted to slide her hands inside his coat and feel his warm skin against hers. To taste his skin on her lips. His frame told her he was big under his clothes, but just how big? Did he have the rippling muscles of a Greek god, or was he lean? She'd seen pictures of naked men in books before, but never a live model. She suddenly blushed.

She gently pulled her hand away. "Lord Blackthorn," she whispered. Her gaze lowered to his lips, then down further, and she suddenly had an urge to undo his cravat and toss it. *Stop this at once*, she chided. She was silent for a few seconds, not really knowing how she should proceed. No doubt he'd had dozens of women at his disposal, and she would be an insignificant nobody if it weren't for the money. He'd never look twice at her otherwise, she knew. The thought was sobering, and it made her remember why she was here in the first place.

She sat down on the chair by the large desk in the middle of the room to put some distance between them. "What did you want to speak to me about?" she said again.

He sat down opposite her. "My solicitor tells me you are interested in Somersby Hall."

"I am," she said.

"It's yours if you are serious about acquiring it."

"Why would I not be serious?" she said, frowning. "Is it because I am a woman?" She was surprised by her own defensiveness and irritation. He had merely asked her if she was serious, and she'd snapped back. The truth was, she was afraid he'd see right through her—her insecurities, her doubts. In turn, she was afraid he would find out the truth of her birth and attempt to circumvent this deal and take all her possessions. She was afraid of losing everything.

"A curious response," he said, raising his brows.

She ignored that remark. *Go ahead, propose the marriage. Do it now before you lose your nerve.* She could hear Kate's words now telling her that it was not going to be easy. "There is something else I must speak to you about—that is, other than Somersby Hall."

His brows rose again. "Oh?"

"I will keep to the point since neither one of us wants to waste any more time than necessary." She stood straighter and looked squarely at him. "I am to inherit a large sum of money . . . quite large, actually. Unfortunately, there are certain stipulations I must adhere to before I can inherit."

His eyes narrowed shrewdly at her. "Let me guess," he said, as if reading her mind. "You need a man with a title?"

The tone of his voice was so condescending. Before she could retort, he said something that really hit a nerve with her.

"Isn't that why a woman such as yourself comes to London for the Season?"

Such as myself? She felt a sudden urge to show him

exactly what kind of woman she was. She took a step forward and looked squarely at him. "And your kind, my lord, will resort to any means necessary to get your hands on a large sum of money, isn't that right?"

"You don't know me well enough to make that assumption."

"I know enough of your kind, my lord," she remarked. "If I had it my way, I wouldn't be here. Believe me when I say that marriage is the last thing I want. God forbid I might aim for greater things in life than to be chattel to an entitled, self-absorbed man." His brows pulled, and his lips thinned, but she wouldn't take it back. "Not that you would comprehend that."

"I wonder, what might have caused you to regard my sex quite severely? Mmm?"

"It's your nature. Your kind can't help yourselves, as it's a trait by default." All the men presented to her at balls had one thing on their minds: *her* inheritance, she thought sullenly. They were all the same, just as the man standing before her. They were privileged yet unwilling to do anything with the power they held in their hands.

Granted, the man before her had managed to assist her, risking his own life in aiding her and Kate, so he must have some measure of decency in him. Still, she was not going to sacrifice everything to answer his questions, only to have him take it all away. She watched him carefully, as his expression was still as stone. It was difficult to read this man, which made this all the harder.

"Present company excluded, for the moment," she said. "You've gone out of your way to assist us, so that much gives you some measure of decency."

"Oh, that makes it so much better," he said sarcastically.

"I mean what I say."

"I am sure you do, in a crude way."

"I'm determined."

His expression hardened. "I will agree with you on that. Determined *and* reckless."

He meant her presence at Whitechapel, but she didn't want him asking more questions than she was willing to answer. "Are we going to conduct our business? Or shall we insult each other some more?"

"Very well. What are the details of this proposal?" he asked.

She watched him carefully, trying to decide how much to reveal. His expression remained hard, causing her to tread carefully. From where she stood, his striking eyes looked deep blue or green, as if she could sink into them. They seemed to change at will, probing her as if he knew exactly what she was thinking. And why had she not noticed his nose that looked as though it had once been broken? Her gaze lowered to his lips, and her heart thumped faster and harder at the thoughts possessing her mind. God, could the man be any more insufferably handsome? She was certain he knew it too, hence his overinflated ego.

"You are correct in that I must marry a man of title to gain my inheritance," she said. "It is also true that I want Somersby Hall, but you must know I don't have the funds to purchase the house now. Once we are wed, I will have access to my entire inheritance." She paused, trying to read his expression, but he gave away nothing. "I am only asking for a year, two at the most. My grandmother's physician thinks she doesn't have much time," she said. "I can draw up a contract which will note that fifty percent of my inheritance and Somersby Hall will be mine; the rest is yours to do with as you wish."

"Fifty percent of what exactly?" he said, his brows rising.

"One hundred thousand pounds, and my grandmother's summer cottage in Wales will be yours, too."

"That's significant," he noted. "Why are you doing this?"

"I already told you."

"Clearly you have properties you can make use of and enough money to be very comfortable for a long time. Why do you want Somersby Hall?"

"I have no wish to remain in Scotland or Wales." *It was a prison to me and is filled with bad memories*, she thought. But instead she said, "Or be handed over to a man without any regards to my wishes. I will not be treated like a chattel."

He narrowed his eyes as if trying to figure out her true motives. "I can understand your need for independence, but chattel? You can easily sell your grandmother's property."

"I don't want the burden of having to sell it after my grandmother's death. In fact, I don't want any part of it, and I don't plan on setting foot in Scotland or Wales again," she said.

"I see." He nodded. "You want to break all ties and start anew."

She nodded. "Will you agree to it or not?" He looked as though he wished to probe further, but he didn't, and she was thankful.

"Who's to say I won't change my mind once we are wed?"

True, and she was scared to death of it, but at this point, she didn't have much choice. It was a risk she must take. "As I have said, from your assistance the other night, I assume you have some measure of honor and decency."

He watched her again with those probing green eyes that seemed to read her thoughts. His gaze lowered to her lips and to her bosom, making her feel extremely discomfited.

"Does this contract include consummating the marriage?"

"Of course not." The thought of such things with this man made her insides tingle with uncertainty. If she wasn't careful, she feared he might see right through her with those sharp eyes of his. "Our arrangement will be strictly business." She paused. "I must tell you that my grandmother has me watched day and night by her loyal companion, Mrs. Pots. This woman would be no less than gratified to see me fail in all regards."

"I see. You despise this woman?"

"It wasn't always that way." Mrs. Pots was a bitter woman, and much of her bitterness was directed at Amelia. "My grandmother has thought of everything, and I am left with few choices."

"To gain your independence." It was a statement rather than a question. "What of your parents?"

"They're dead." Her father was dead. Even if her mother was alive, she'd never made any attempt to contact her. Sudden hot anger and resentment burned through her. She didn't like this. She didn't want to feel this feeling that always seemed to cloud her mind. "I don't have much time. I need an answer."

Chapter 9

HELL, HE WAS going to regret this.

Marriage in exchange for her inheritance? A very significant sum at that. This woman must be desperate to give away so much in exchange for her independence, as she called it. Marriage was the last thing he wanted, but this agreement fit his needs well. He could not afford to not agree to her contract. The money would help remedy his father's debt, settle his mother in a comfortable living, and allow him to leave London for good.

"You understand that I don't plan on staying in London for long."

"I expect you to stay the Season."

"With you?"

"Not with me, no. But surely you realize we must be seen together to convince the *ton* we are husband and wife."

"Yes, I suppose that can't be helped."

She frowned. "You must know, I don't enjoy this. If I could somehow gain my independence on my own, I would, but I can't. I have planned this for too long to simply give it up, so I'd appreciate it if you could cooperate and pretend, at least, you aren't repulsed by my presence."

He walked over to her and she backed away. He looked deeply into her eyes. God, if only she knew how he wanted to bed her right now, to see her coiffed hair wild and free. "Believe me, that is not what's on my mind right now." He took her hand and kissed the knuckles, one by one. "Quite the opposite. You are feisty and reckless, yes. Repulsed by you? Far from it, my sweet." He offered her a smile, and he saw the seductive heat fill her eyes. This knowledge that she wasn't immune to his charm pleased him a great deal.

"Oh," she said, pulling her hand away. "Good."

His smile faded. "One more thing . . ."

Her expression tensed. The quiet beauty looked back at him with uncertainty in her brown eyes. He hardly knew this woman standing before him, but there was a sense of fragility about her, one he hadn't noticed until now.

Strands of blond hair escaped the confines of her bun and hung loose like a waterfall. His finger itched to stroke it and move further down to the hills of her perfect bosom. Her brows pulled, questions lingering in those eyes. His mind listed all the obvious reasons he shouldn't agree to her scheme, but reality left him with very little choice.

"If I am going to agree to your proposal," he said, "I need you to answer some questions." What the hell was she thinking walking into the devil's den in the middle of the night?

She nodded wearily. Good, at least she was smart enough not to fight him on this.

"Why were you at St. Giles? It's full of murderers and thugs."

She frowned. At times, there was something in her eyes that was . . . sad . . . cautious. Or maybe angry? "I was looking for someone," she finally said.

"Who were you looking for?" The fight in her eyes told him she wasn't willing to give it up so easily. Should he be concerned? He wasn't certain. "I need to know what I am getting myself into if I choose to go along with this scheme."

"Scheme?" she said. "Is that what you think this is? This has far more importance than that, not that you would understand."

"Help me understand, then."

"Why must you be so insistent? You have no concern in this. You will gain a fortune for this so-called 'scheme,' my lord."

He sighed. "I have met you in the most precarious circumstances, which makes me question your motive. I must insist you answer if we are to move forward." *Bloody hell, just take the money and go your separate ways*, his mind ordered.

She sighed in defiance. "I was looking for a friend."

Looking for a friend at East End? Interesting, indeed. "And this friend of yours, is she in some sort of predicament I need to be aware of?"

She paused, watching him carefully. "I don't know."

"That man in the alley, what did he want with you?"

"I don't know."

He watched her expression, every twitch, the pull of her

lips downward, just enough to tell him she didn't know if he could be trusted.

"You needn't worry," she told him. "I will be fine. Besides, I am certain the inheritance will remedy any inconvenience to you."

"I am not sure about that," he whispered. "I will consider your proposal." *You need the damn money and you know it.* In all truth, his gut told him to walk away, but he didn't have much choice at the moment.

"You will?" she said. "A serious consideration?"

"I said I would, didn't I?" He watched her expression again, the soft glow of the candlelight softening her features. "I will give you my answer within the week."

She frowned. "I don't have the luxury of time."

"I will endeavor to give you my answer sooner," he said with a nod.

"I will give you two days," she said boldly. "Two days, my lord. Good night, Lord Blackthorn." With that, she walked out of the study and closed the door with a click.

Chapter 10

AMELIA SLIPPED OUT of the library and closed the door behind her. With her hand on her chest, she willed her heart to slow. She let out a long sigh, welcoming a deep sense of relief. The meeting, she concluded, had been a good start.

A very good start.

And most importantly, the hard part was over. A sense of accomplishment ensued. She hadn't realized the tremendous pressure she had been under until this moment had passed and relief washed over her. She hadn't thought about all the things that could have gone wrong until now. Perhaps it had been too awful to even consider. Still, there was much to accomplish before she could finally be free.

There was something else, this strange feeling that came over her every time she was in the presence of the earl. It wasn't the same feeling she'd felt for the stable hand who had become more than her friend.

Many years ago, he had found her sobbing in one of the stalls after she'd been reprimanded for not finishing her lesson and for talking back to Mrs. Pots. She'd been young, and so had he, and from there, their friendship had grown and blossomed. There were a few stolen kisses and promises she could never keep, and their private moment each day, however short, was the only thing she had looked forward to. But her grandmother had discovered the truth and punished them.

Warm tears wet her cheeks, but she wiped them away. She wondered where the stable hand was now. She owed him much.

But this feeling for the earl wasn't as simple, and she didn't like it. It made her second-guess herself in his presence and think of him in a most disturbing manner that made her want.

She had dreamt of this moment for so many years, secretly planning how she would one day return to London and reunite with Millie. After all, she'd promised to do so, hadn't she?

While her grandmother had been relentless in her demands, Amelia had known that if she abided by her wishes long enough, she would gain her grandmother's trust and have the chance to ensure her own freedom—far from the misery of her childhood and a future shackled like a slave to fulfill the wishes of men, just as her mother had been. No, she was not going to be that woman.

Stepping away from the door, she quickly she made her way to the ballroom before Mrs. Pots could notice her missing. As soon as she entered the ballroom, she saw Mrs. Pots searching in the crowd for her.

Blast. She quickly made her way through the crowd, hoping Mrs. Pots hadn't seen her enter the ballroom. She nudged her way between large crowds of people conversing along the periphery. She saw a large palm, and she backed into the wall toward it, where she nearly collided with a woman.

"Pardon," Amelia said. "I did not see you there."

The young woman swiped at her dress. Quite young. Perhaps this was her first Season? She looked up at Amelia not with contempt, but with a smile, as if to undo the tension. There was something in her eyes that was kind, humble, and Amelia instantly took a liking to her.

"Oh, heavens," the young woman said. "It was my fault, really. I should have seen you coming."

Amelia felt horrified as she looked down at the woman's lovely dress, a very expensive one at that. "I am afraid we will need to get the stain off your dress."

The young woman looked down at her dress dotted with red punch. "Oh," she said. "My brother will be furious with me."

"I am sorry, really I am."

The young woman smiled, as if to concede. "Actually, you did me a great service. However, I am afraid my brother will be most disappointed."

"Your brother?"

"Oh," she said. "My apologies. I'm Emily Wentworth." She dipped down suddenly.

"What is the matter?"

"My brother, there, is the Duke of Kemp."

The Duke of Kemp. Amelia had heard of him once or twice. She saw a handsome man looking in her direction and she gave him a faint smile. His frown transformed into a wide smile. If she recalled from what Kate had told her, the Duke of Kemp was married to an American heiress who had doubled his fortune. There were rumors that she could not give the duke a son, and that he may proceed with a divorce.

"I'm Amelia Knight," she said. "I am very sorry about your dress."

The woman's eyes widened. "You're the heiress from Scotland, are you not?"

"Don't hold that against me."

Miss Wentworth chuckled, and several women glared at them disapprovingly. Amelia looked back and, standing on her tiptoes, searched the crowd.

"If you don't mind me asking, who are you hiding from?"

"My chaperone. I don't think she sees me yet, which is a good thing, I suppose. She's there," Amelia said, her eyes directing her newfound friend to the crowd where couples were engaged in a waltz.

Miss Wentworth observed the older woman looking about the crowd. "She reminds me of a prickly thorn."

Amelia held back a laugh to avoid attention. "Why are you hiding from the duke, if you don't mind me asking?"

Miss Wentworth sighed. "My brother is in the process of procuring a husband for me."

Amelia understood that all too well. "His grace will not allow you the choice?"

Miss Wentworth's smile faded. "Even if he did, do we really have a choice in the matter?"

There was a sense of defeat in Miss Wentworth's tone. Before Amelia could respond, the clank of glass hushed the entire room, and Amelia and Miss Wentworth both went still. To Amelia's surprise, the Earl Blackthorn was standing near the orchestra holding a glass of champagne, as if he were about to make an important announcement.

"It's the Earl Blackthorn," Miss Wentworth said, tiptoeing to see what was happening. "Maybe he has proposed marriage to the Countess Deveraux. I heard she is back in London."

Was that the woman Amelia had seen in the library earlier during the ball when his lordship had asked her to meet him? Could this woman be the reason for his reluctance to agree to her plan? Was he still in love with her? Perhaps he had changed his mind in the last few minutes since Amelia had left him in the library. A fickle man. Strange, he didn't seem like the sort, she thought with deep disappointment seeping into her heart.

"Dear friends," Earl Blackthorn started. What on earth was he doing now? She moved an inch closer to listen. "Tonight I have the pleasure of introducing you to a very special woman."

Amelia looked around the room, biting her lip, afraid to listen further. Her heart pumped faster as each second ticked by.

"Miss Amelia Knight," he finally said. "My fiancée."

Amelia froze unable to speak or comprehend what was happening. What on earth? Did he just say her name to the *ton*? Plastering a smile on her face, she whispered, "Oh, no, no, no." Oh, God, what was happening? Was he mad?

Gasps and whispers waved through the ballroom. All eyes turned toward where she stood, foolishly standing there, unable to move.

Blackthorn's mother was by his side, smiling. "Where is the lovely bride-to-be?"

The crowd fell silent and parted.

A wide smile came over Miss Wentworth, surprise flickering in her eyes. "Go," she said, nudging Amelia. "You can't deny Lord Blackthorn."

She started to move. Why was she so nervous? This was what she had wanted all along. She felt all the eyes in the room on her, and this made her quite uncomfortable. She didn't like crowds, not in the least.

When she joined him near the orchestra, he said, "Would you do me the honor of dancing with me, my sweet?"

She smiled and nodded rigidly.

They proceeded to the dance floor as the orchestra played a waltz. He cupped his warm hand around her right hand and placed the other on her back, and as they moved, he proceeded to pull her close to him and lead the waltz. The man moved as smoothly as if he had done this a million times. His footsteps glided easily without a hitch, and she followed his lead just the way she had been taught.

The music filled the air, and he pressed her close, while he whirled her around the room like a silk ribbon fluttering in the wind. All the while, he had full control of every turn, every movement.

Heart pumping with excitement as if she were a giddy girl, she reminded herself this was just part of the business deal. His eyes were on her as if nothing else mattered, and she dared not look away. She needed the crowd to think they were in love, a good suitable match. Even though she would have gladly simply paid him for the house and been left alone to do as she wished, that was not a choice she had.

The whispers and murmurs from the crowd made her uneasy. It wasn't that she didn't like people, indeed she had met some decent people, but they weren't this kind of people. The people she enjoyed were decent, hardworking individuals that knew the value of human life. These people valued one thing and one thing only: money. She could see their scrutiny as if she were some specimen to be dissected.

She knew her duty, and she had been trained well. This was the price she had to pay to accomplish what she had dreamt of for nearly all her life. In the corner, she saw Miss Wentworth smile at her, making the situation a little more bearable. Still, she must have looked nervous, because Blackthorn tipped her chin to look at him.

"Don't mind them. Keep your eyes on me," he said, then whispered in her ear, "You look beautiful."

He swirled her around once more. Her heart beat faster with each swirl, touch, and glance as if she might believe she was the princess being wooed by the prince. Far from it.

Her gaze met his for several seconds, and his expression was unreadable. Then his lips formed a reassuring smile that said everything was going to be fine. It made her feel wanted, safe in his arms, allowing her doubt to slowly dissolve.

Another turn. Then another.

Before she could get her head around what was happening, the music came to a stop. He gently tugged her to him, quite close, lifted her hand to his lips, and kissed it. Sounds of "ah" and gasps followed from the crowd.

She pulled her gaze away and looked at the crowd gathering, whispering. But he pulled her to him, forcing her to look at him. What was happening? And why had he announced their engagement without notifying her? Before she had the chance to say something, the earl invited the crowd to dance.

"Shall we take refreshments?"

She nodded, touching her chest and feeling her heart pumping wildly. As they stepped off the dance floor, her hand slipped through the crook of his arm and rested there as he led her away from the crowd toward the refreshments table opposite the French doors. They didn't exchange words. As strange as it was, being near the earl made the night a little easier, as long as he didn't try to take control of the situation.

All of a sudden, she grew resentful.

Very resentful.

Chapter 11

BLACKTHORN ESCORTED MISS Knight out of the ballroom and into the rose garden to escape the crowd and give him time to question her further.

He'd done things on a whim before, but the proposal was uncharacteristic of him. Granted, he'd had to adjust to situations quickly when living on the fringe of danger, but this? He'd never made a rash decision that would shave nearly two years off his life.

Why had he been so rash in his decision to announce the engagement tonight?

Was it because the men had gawked at her, watching her move about the room with interest in their eyes? Oh, he had noticed it all right. To his annoyance. Even Grayson had seemed too happy in her presence. Or was it watching Kendall leave the ball with a look of warning? Thirty days, he had said.

Only thirty days.

The air seemed a little warm this evening, and the stars

were bright. When was the last time he had seen stars, or looked up at the sky in contemplation? His behavior had been very uncharacteristic as of late. Then he looked at the woman walking next to him. She said nothing. Probably concocting something spiteful to say to him.

She looked squarely at him. "What was that about?" she questioned. "I distinctly recall you weren't ready to give me an answer."

Of course she'd get right to the point of the matter. Still, he found her frankness refreshing, despite her prickly disposition. "I thought you'd rather be pleased."

She frowned. "Pleased?" she started. "I am pleased that you have agreed to the arrangement. However, I would have preferred the courtesy of knowing your intentions before you announced it to everyone."

Her lips thinned in anger, then her face eased as she gazed beyond where he stood. She stood on her tiptoes to look around.

"What's the matter?" he said, looking in the same direction.

"I thought I saw someone," she blurted out. An aged couple near them smiled, then continued on their way. She shook her head as if frustrated. "You should have informed me before announcing our engagement to the world."

"It wasn't the world," he said. "And I thought this was what you wanted."

Her brows rose in question. When he said nothing, she continued. "I do like to be part of the decision-making process. Perhaps I made a mistake in coming to you with this arrangement."

"You're angry," he said, his brows rising in amusement. He saw her glare at him with burning eyes. "Again."

"Yes, I am, rightfully so," she said firmly. "Just because you are a man doesn't give you the right to make the decision for me. I have told you, I will be an equal partner in this; otherwise, I shall have no choice but to move on to the next candidate."

"I am sorry if I have upset you," he said quietly. "It was not my intention."

There was a sense of raw vulnerability in her tone, and her eyes filled with controlled fire. His reaction to this was rather perplexing, as he fought the compulsion to hold her in his arms, to kiss away the tension between them. She stood perfectly still as if determined to win the conversation, her eyes cold and proud. Then her defensiveness slowly began to subside.

She looked away. "Please don't look at me like that," she said.

"How am I looking at you?" He told himself he'd use this time to find out more about her. After all, he had to protect his interest since she wasn't volunteering the information he sought from her about the night he'd found her in the alley with a very dangerous man.

"You stare at me with such intensity. It's quite unnerving, you realize," she said softly, giving him a wary glance.

Quite unlike him, he said, "Then I shall endeavor to do my best not to."

She lifted her chin as if finding her strength once more. "You needn't pretend there is actually something meaningful between us when we are alone."

Was he pretending? Carried away by his own desires, he leaned in close. His voice almost at a whisper, he said, "We are going to marry, and for the duration of that period, you are my responsibility." He placed his hand on her elbow and pulled her to him. Leaning forward, he gently kissed her cheek, and she didn't stop him.

Her gaze met his and remained there for a moment. He wanted to kiss her desperately. Jesus, her skin felt delectably soft. His hand lifted to cup her neck, and she slowly leaned into him, not resisting. He liked this. Oh yeah, his body was reaching to her even before he could get his head around what was happening. Their eyes locked, and desire brewed in her beautiful brown eyes that reminded him of chocolate. Then she quickly pulled away.

She remained still, observing him as she had done numerous times. "I have to go; my chaperone must be looking for me."

"It is customary for the bride-to-be to meet with the guests and accept their congratulations before she departs." Since when did he care about his family tradition? This was Max's territory, but then again, Max was no longer here.

"Oh," she said. "I don't suppose you'd tell them I'm suffering a headache?"

"I could, but how will that serve us if we are to convince them the union is genuine?"

She bit her lower lip and contemplated. "I suppose you are right." Then she became quiet, thinking for several seconds. "Actually, there is something I'd like to ask you."

"Go on," he said.

"I hear you were in his majesty's army. Is that true?"

He nodded. "But only for a short time." He'd been in the army when he was recruited to spy for his country, but he preferred to keep that information to himself if possible.

"Oh," she said, stopping short in dismay.

"Why are you asking this?" he asked, intrigued.

"I just thought you seemed to have more experience from the way you handled those hoodlums in the alley."

What was she getting at? "And if I do?"

Her eyes shone with delight. "How much experience, exactly?"

"Enough. Why?"

"I . . ." She hesitated as if she shouldn't say more. "I need some assistance finding my friend. I have tried since arriving in London, and I am not having much success. It will be dangerous, as you already discovered the other night. I fear Millie may be in the hands of thugs, or even worse, back with her father." She paused, as if reflecting on her past. "He can be cruel . . . very cruel, actually."

"And you feel I can use my fists to get your friend back?"

"If need be, yes." She paused, watching his expression. It seemed he didn't look disagreeable to what she had just revealed to him. "I must insist that I am included in this endeavor, as I am an equal partner in this."

"Does this mean the deal is off if I decline to help find your friend?"

"Of course not," she said. "But I do hope you'll consider it. If you want additional sums from my portion, I am willing to—"

"I don't need additional funds," he remarked. "We agreed to split it fifty-fifty."

"And don't forget Somersby Hall."

"Once we are wed and I get my portion, you can have the property."

She smiled at his response. "Good."

The smile in her eyes squeezed his chest. "You should do that more often."

"Do what?"

"Smile," he said. "It suits you."

She looked away shyly. He touched her cheek with his thumb and rubbed across it. She cupped his hand and held it in hers, then slowly dropped it. Oh hell, he wanted to kiss her, and for a single moment he thought she would let him. Instead, she dropped her gaze and looked away.

"I think it will be best to procure a special license and wed as soon as possible," he said.

"I do too, the sooner the better."

"I will need several days to acquire the special license. In the meantime, we can get started looking for your friend."

"You should be aware my grandmother expects you to present yourself after we wed."

"I see," he said. "I will need to make travel plans for us, then." She seemed nervous, unsure. "What is it?"

Her expression was full of worry. "It's just happening so fast. If you don't require my company, I'd like to go home."

"I thought I'd introduce you to the other guests."

"Must I?" she said. "I am rather tired and would like to rest if you don't mind."

"I can take you home now, if you wish it."

"Thank you," she said. "But I can see to it myself."

He watched her for several seconds, and she had an inkling that he was going to insist on escorting her home. She had already spent too much of her time with this man, granted for a good cause, but it was beginning to feel . . . complicated, and she wanted to keep it simple between them.

"Besides, the less time we spend together than necessary, the better, I think," she said.

She didn't have the room for contemplating this man. This big, capable man that made her want and desire things that she shouldn't; she didn't have that kind of indulgence in her life. Her own freedom was at stake, and she had bigger things to worry about, like finding Millie. This thought helped her sober up.

"You're right," he said. "The less complicated this is, the better."

Chapter 12

BLACKTHORN WASN'T IMMUNE to beauty.

Now that they were engaged, a sense of fierce possessiveness suddenly gripped him, surprising him. He watched Miss Knight depart with trepidation. He'd had his share of women here in England and abroad, but with her, he felt this unyielding conflict within him.

While she spoke of independence and having her own income, there was a feeling of vulnerability. Was he discerning more than was there?

One thing was certain, this woman aroused and vexed him, far more than he liked on so many levels. If he had his way, he'd swoop her up in his arms and take her to his bed, but he couldn't. He wouldn't. He didn't want to complicate this any more than she did. He meant to keep this transaction simple and get the hell of out London. Which meant he needed to settle the debt to Kendall.

After returning home, he did some more digging on Kendall. His informants went far and deep among the underground criminals of London, so when he discovered Andrew Kendall had grown up in the streets in Whitechapel until about age twelve, he wasn't surprised. A man like Kendall knew how to manipulate his opponent and the weak to his advantage, no matter who he hurt.

It seemed Kendall had disappeared for a decade during his teen years. Blackthorn's sources indicated Kendall may have gone abroad, maybe even selling stolen goods and pirating. When he'd returned, he'd bought a townhouse in Mayfair and married the daughter of a wealthy merchant before opening a private gambling hall that had expanded.

The money owed by Blackthorn's father was legitimate, from what he'd been told by his sources. To stave off gossip and embarrassment, his father had asked Kendall to keep this quiet and give him time to pay off the debt. Kendall had agreed with twenty percent interest added to what was already owed, to which Blackthorn's father had agreed.

Max had known about the debt, but before he could intervene, he had passed from a fever. Within a week, their father had suffered a heart attack and died instantly.

Their father had been a damn, bloody fool.

Upon returning home after the ball, Mrs. Pots informed Amelia that she would need a day to take care of some matters, to which Amelia happily agreed. Perhaps the woman realized that now that Amelia was engaged, Mrs. Pots had no power over her, as she would have to face Lord Blackthorn too.

Now, Amelia sat by the fireplace after her maid had helped her undress to retire for the evening. Her legs tucked underneath her night-rail, she watched the fire in the hearth and exhaled. She'd accomplished what she needed to tonight, she thought with a sense of pride and relief.

She felt very relieved, actually.

Now the only thing she needed to focus on was making certain her grandmother didn't find out what she was up to. Which meant she needed to make certain Society believed that the engagement was the real thing and keep Mrs. Pots from snooping around.

Since last night, Mrs. Pots had been occupied. With what, Amelia wasn't certain, but she welcomed it. She sighed in relief. With Lord Blackthorn's help, she hoped she would hear some good news.

Lord Blackthorn, she thought, feeling the warmth of the fire burning hot. He had spoken of consummating the marriage, and of course she had told him exactly what she thought of that idea.

Secretly, she may indulge, but in reality, intimacy with him would be a grave mistake. Just being in his presence made her doubt herself and her secret longing that could never come to light. To stave off these illicit thoughts, she thought of his mistress yesterday.

Actually, if she was completely honest, Blackthorn and Zara made a flawless couple, she thought with a pang of jealousy. They were perfect for each other, and if he chose to take Zara to bed, then it was none of her affair. Better yet, she thought he should; that would surely put an end to her lustful thoughts of the man.

Would he go to Zara after the wedding and make love to her?

Why wouldn't he?

Amelia had already informed him what he did with other women was not her concern as long as he was discreet. But she secretly could not deny the disappointment she would feel if he did bed another. She'd be very disappointed.

A quick knock alerted her, and she jumped in her seat. The door swung opened. It didn't surprise her. When she had first come to live with her grandmother in Scotland, it had been difficult with Mrs. Pots relentlessly ordering her about. She'd had no privacy and if she did, it wasn't for very long, as Mrs. Pots would find her hiding in a corner reading or scribbling in her journal. Now it was part of her world and she had learned to ignore her.

Mrs. Pots stood by the doorframe and observed her. More like a glare, but she was in a good mood tonight.

"I'll be writing to your grandmother about tonight," the woman said.

"Good," Amelia said, as if what Mrs. Pots had said was nothing special. "You will save me the trouble of doing so myself." She looked up at the older woman.

Mrs. Pots added, "And I will be addressing the concerns I have of your behavior as of late."

Amelia glared at her. "What behavior?" she asked. "I chose the man she wanted me to marry. I am certain she will be more than happy with my choice."

"It's not what you did. It's what you are not saying. I can

feel it in my bones. You're up to something." Her chaperone watched Amelia carefully before she turned on her heel and left the room.

Oh, the dreadful woman.

Mrs. Pots' footfalls slowly faded down the hall. From the day Amelia had arrived at her grandmother's house, the woman had been hostile to her, as if she had the right to be so. No matter what she did or didn't do, Mrs. Pots would find something to chide her or punish—

A shattering sound jerked her out of her thoughts, then a loud thud on the carpeted floor prompted her to stand. Her head whisked around to see a fist-size rock on the carpet. It had happened so fast that she just stood there staring at it, unable to move. Glancing at the shattered window with tiny pieces of broken glass beneath it, she froze.

Heart pounding.

Then she saw something strange from the corner of her eye. There was a piece of paper secured to the rock by a black ribbon. Clearly, this was no accident. She looked at the window and waited to make certain nothing else was going to be tossed into her room. Then she heard quick footfalls above her where Mrs. Pots' room was located.

Quickly retrieving the stone, she hid it behind her pillow. Within seconds, there was a quick knock. Kate slipped in quietly and looked at the broken window, then at the shattered glass on the carpet.

"Well, that explains the noise," she said, walking up to the window, avoiding the shards of broken glass.

"Help me. I don't want Mrs. Pots to find this."

Quickly, both women picked up the glass one piece at a time and gathered it in the corner of the room where it was not visible from the door. When there was a knock at the door and it flung open, Amelia closed the curtains just in time.

Mrs. Pots glared at both woman suspiciously. "What troubles are you concocting in here?" she blurted out. "I heard noises."

"Trouble?" Amelia said. "We were just conversing about the . . . um . . . engagement."

Kate's eyes widened, but she quickly nodded with excitement. "It's going to be such a grand wedding," Kate said, smiling widely.

"Why do I get the feeling you are hiding something from me?" Mrs. Pots said.

"All right. It was me," Kate said, sighing. "Silly girl that I am. I could not maintain my exuberance and dropped my book that I had in my hand when she told me of the news."

"Book?" Mrs. Pots said suspiciously. "I have never had the occasion to see you with a book."

"Well, I have taken up reading and studying, if you must know. I quite enjoy it," Kate said with a smirk.

Mrs. Pots narrowed her eyes, and Amelia's heart thumped. If she chose to investigate and saw the shards of glass or opened the curtain, there was going to be explaining to do.

"What I heard wasn't a thump."

"All right," Kate said, throwing her arms in the air as if exasperated. "If you insist on knowing the truth, I have an admirer. He's quite angry at me for avoiding him, you see. He came here to try to get my attention and profess his love to me by throwing pebbles at my window. I guess the pebble was more like a small rock." Kate opened the curtain to show her the shattered window.

Mrs. Pots eyed her suspiciously. "Why would he be throwing pebbles in this room?"

"Who knows what he may be thinking?" Kate said, frowning. "The man isn't known for his intelligence, although I must say, his looks quite make up for that lack, if you know what I mean."

Mrs. Pots glared at them with doubt in her eyes. "Make sure the housekeeper takes care of that." Then she gave them another suspicious look and left the room.

Both women exhaled.

"That was close," Kate said. "What happened?"

Amelia walked over to her bed and lifted her pillow. Taking out the rock, she pulled the note loose from the ribbon. Both women took no time in unfolding the paper and reading it together: *Do not attempt to look for Millie. This is your only warning.*

The two women looked at each other.

Finally, Kate spoke. "What will you do?"

Chapter 13

AMELIA AWOKE IN her room the next morning heaving and touching her chest, her heart pumping wildly, and her heightened senses arousing her. She kept her eyes closed for fear the dream might dissolve into nothingness.

Lust, this wicked ache for him, was maddening as she felt the heat between her legs. The excitement bombarded her as if she were deprived of human contact. In truth, she had been deprived of everything for so long.

Opening her eyes, she replayed her dream in her mind. Lord Blackthorn was nude in all his glory, seducing her and promising her things she dared not repeat out loud. He caressed every crevice, every part of her body with soft kisses, and she begged him not to stop as he lowered himself farther until he reached the apex of her sex, his tongue caressing the hot spot. Oh, how her body ached for him; that is, until he suddenly turned into a giant serpent and proceeded to swallow her whole.

What the bloody hell did this mean?

That he couldn't be trusted? All the doubts and worries she kept deep in her heart surfaced in one big wave of emotion. What if he changed his mind about their agreement? What if he demanded children? What if he challenged the marriage contract between them in court and demanded all of her money?

What if, what if, what if . . .

Could he do that? She wasn't certain, but what she did know was this line of questioning was only going to make her worry to no end. Besides, she knew this would be a risk she had no choice in taking.

She must keep her wits about her. All that mattered was that she got her portion of the inheritance and the house, so she could make it a home for herself.

In the end, she settled her mind and closed her eyes, thinking about Lord Blackthorn. She lay in her bed for several more minutes and when no relief came she pulled on the tassel for her maid. Once her maid arrived and helped her dress, she had the footman deliver a note to Lord Blackthorn. If she was going to allow him to help her with finding Millie, she needed to be honest with him in all regards.

She rang for Mrs. Pots and told her she was going to have breakfast in her room and would like to be left alone to recover from last night. The woman slapped Amelia's schedule for the day on her desk and instructed that the day's lesson was to be turned in before noon.

Amelia quickly informed her chaperone that since she was now officially engaged, she no longer needed to keep to Mrs. Pots' instructions. The woman glared at her, her lips thinning in displeasure.

"I don't recall your grandmother giving me that instruction."

"You are welcome to write to her, if you wish," Amelia said. "You may even address my fiancé regarding this matter if you like."

Mrs. Pots' lips thinned even further. She glared at Amelia and walked out of her room. That was close. Amelia doubted the woman would approach the lord, and if she chose to write to her grandmother, she was free to do so. By then, all this matter would be resolved.

Shortly after she finished her breakfast, Lord Blackthorn arrived. She started to feel strangely nervous and anxious. Her stomach felt tight, and she had difficulty concentrating. Instead of anticipating the meeting, the images of him naked and seducing her kept popping up in her head.

This was not helping.

She heard someone slip into her room with a click of the door. She gasped as Lord Blackthorn's finger touched his lips in a gesture to remain quiet. Swiftly, he walked over to her. How had he come in here without being noticed? There was something alert and purposeful about his steps as he joined her.

"I got the note," he said, pulling the thick curtains open and looking at the broken window. "Are you hurt?"

"No," she whispered. "If you could keep your voice quiet," she said, leading him to the stairs. "I don't want Mrs. Pots to know about your presence. How did you get in here without being noticed, anyway?"

"I have my ways," he said. "Show me the rest."

She walked over to the drawer next to her bed and pulled out the large rock with the note that had been attached to it.

Lord Blackthorn's sharp gaze seemed to miss nothing. Then he studied the note. "Left-handed," he muttered.

"Pardon?" she asked.

"This individual is left-handed."

"How do you know this?"

"See the way this letter curves just so?" he said, pointing to one of the letters on the note. He carefully placed the evidence in his coat pocket. "Is there anything else I need to know?"

"That is all I have for you."

"You can't stay here," he said. "Is there someone in town you can stay with?"

"I don't know anyone here in town except Kate."

"That does present a problem, doesn't it?" he said, his brow raised.

"It does, indeed. Mrs. Pots will be very suspicious, and I can't risk that. Besides, this townhouse is paid for the entire Season."

"I agree in that regard; however, you are clearly not safe here."

"I have to remain here," she insisted. "I can't afford Mrs. Pots informing my grandmother that I have taken residence elsewhere."

"Well, if that is the case, I can have someone scour the neighborhood at night and keep an eye on the house."

"Who is this person?"

"His name is Kane Roberts, a Bow Street Runner. We served together in the war."

"And you trust him?"

"I do."

"I don't know," she said. "It doesn't ease my mind knowing some strange man is lurking about my house."

"All right, then, it's either me or Roberts. Take your pick."

"Is this really necessary?" she asked. This man was really bent on securing his investment, wasn't he? "I only thought the note might help us in finding Millie."

"You *will* need to choose," he said. "I have a vested interest in your safety, remember."

Of course he'd say that. Still, the thought of this man in her room at night didn't sit well with her. If she agreed to have Mr. Roberts scour the streets and Mrs. Pots discovered him, she would be done for. And if she found Lord Blackthorn in her room, Mrs. Pots would surely inform her grandmother too. "Can you assure me that you will make certain no one sees you here?"

"I got into the house unnoticed, didn't I?"

"Yes, you did," she said, narrowing her eyes suspiciously. He said nothing.

"Fine, you can stay," she said. "Don't expect me to entertain you."

"Believe me, if I didn't have to be here, I wouldn't be," he said.

She didn't give him the pleasure of responding to his remark. In fact, she ignored it. Instead she said, "Have you thought of a plan to find Millie?" The look on his face told her he might have, but he said nothing to her. "If you discovered something, I would like to know. Remember, I indicated that this was an equal partnership, and I meant it."

"I have," he said. "But I will need to inquire on my own."

"You have information regarding Millie? You know where she is?"

"I might," he said.

"I will go with you."

"No, you won't."

"Yes, I am going with you," she said firmly. "I insist on it. This is what we agreed on."

"Bloody hell, you're going to get yourself really hurt one of these days."

"But not before you collect your money, is that it?"

"Don't say I didn't warn you."

"Thank you for your concern, my lord," she said sarcastically. "But I don't scare easily."

"So you keep insisting," he said. "Meet me outside in thirty minutes."

Before she could respond, he slipped out of the room just as easily as he'd come in. How did the man do that? This man certainly had many skills that surprised her.

She quickly looked herself over in the long oval mirror and when she was satisfied, she left her room and started to walk down the stairs. Even before she reached the bottom, Mrs. Pots was giving orders as if she owned the place.

Amelia saw the spectacle. Mrs. Pots was directing footmen carrying vases of red roses into the house. The flowers were breathtaking, and the aroma was lovely.

She'd never seen so many, never mind in one room. Her grandmother insisted on cleanliness, and that included not having unnecessary frivolous items in the house, which included flowers.

"What is all this?" Amelia asked, taking in the fragrance of the roses in the hallway.

Mrs. Pots turned to her and said, "You tell me." Handing her a small envelope, she instructed another footman to place the flowers in the parlor. "No, no, young man," she said when he tried to put the vase on the center table in the foyer. "I told you, in the parlor." She pointed to the hallway.

Amelia opened the envelope: *For my lovely bride-to-be. Blackthorn.*

When had he arranged all this? A tingling sensation bubbled inside her tummy, spreading outward like sunshine. Why had he sent these flowers? Amelia wondered. To convince Society they were in love? Of course, why else would he send them?

"I can guess who it is from." Mrs. Pots paused to direct the footman again. "What does it say?" She leaned over to get a glimpse of the card.

"Don't you have something to occupy your time besides going through my personal things?"

Mrs. Pots narrowed her eyes, frowning. "I was hired to do just that. Until you say 'I do,' it is my business to make certain you don't make a fool of yourself and disgrace your family. Nor will I have you making a fool of your grandmother."

Amelia felt the carefully tucked-away emotions of her

past slowly erupting from deep inside her. The woman had not a single kind word to say to her, or to anyone for that matter. Women like her always had ulterior motives; Amelia knew that much from her own experience. Unless it benefitted her chaperone one way or another, she wouldn't lift a finger. "What has my grandmother promised you?"

The woman said nothing.

"I caution you, Mrs. Pots. If I must, I will remove you from this house. You'll have no choice but to crawl back to my grandmother and explain why you couldn't do the job you were hired to do." Damn, she hated to do that, but the woman was dreadful. "I will be going out. You will not be chaperoning me today. I will have Mrs. McBride with me." Amelia turned on her heel and walked up the stairs to retrieve her bonnet and gloves to meet Lord Blackthorn.

She told herself to keep walking and not turn back before the dreadful woman stopped her. Her heart thumped harder and faster. This was the first time she'd stood up to the woman in this manner, and she was afraid that if she stopped walking, she'd lose her nerve.

Keep walking, Amelia . . .

Thirty minutes later, Blackthorn and Amelia were in an unmarked carriage on their way to look for Millie. The truth was, young women like Millie Penn most often disappeared for two reasons.

They were either dead or in prison.

The last time he was here, he'd been a prisoner, posing

as a thief in order to gain sensitive information that would help the war against Napoleon. What was supposed to be a week long mission had turned into nearly a month.

"Where are we?" Amelia asked, breaking into his thoughts.

He looked out the window and stared at the large gray building with iron bars around the entrance. Dark smoke rose from the grimy, sooted chimney above, seeping into the gray clouds. This dreary place was no place for Amelia, but she had insisted on being part of all this.

"Newgate Prison." Sudden primal need gripped him, the need to protect this fragile, angelic beauty. As soon as he opened the carriage door, the stench bombarded him with memories he had long buried. He stepped down and his polished boots hit the mud. Thick from the rain, it spattered the dark leather.

"What are we doing here?" she asked. "You don't suppose . . ." Her voice trailed off as realization dawned, and she went pale.

"It's just a hunch," he said. "Wait for me in the carriage."

She shook her head. "No," she said. "If she is in there, I want to see her."

Reluctantly, he helped her out of the carriage and saw her expression churn. She quietly followed him, and once they reached the front entrance, he stopped. There was a small rectangular lookout on the iron door. He lifted the knocker and alerted the guard.

When no one came, he banged on the door with his fist. It was still early; everyone must be in the back guarding the prisoners during breakfast. A few seconds later, weary eyes came into view.

"Wot do ye want?" The guard glared at Blackthorn, but grinned when he saw Amelia. The look in the guard's eyes was nothing but lascivious as his gaze lowered to her bosom.

Blackthorn felt her scoot closer to him. He lifted his hands and gave the guard several shiny coins through the lookout. The guard took them, and the door squeaked open.

"I need to see a prisoner," Blackthorn said. "Millie Penn."

The guard's brows furrowed in a frown. "Fer wot reason?"

Blackthorn was certain most of these guards didn't know all the prisoners by name, so he took his chance. "She is my client, and I am here on behalf of her family."

"Yer a solicitor, are ye?" he said, looking Blackthorn over and then looking at Amelia. Solicitors did not often visit these prisoners, and if they did enter the rodent- and disease-ridden prison, it was to rob the unfortunate souls for their own gain.

"I am."

"And her, who is she?"

"Her sister," Blackthorn lied.

He frowned. "Stay here." The guard slammed the door.

"You just lied to that man," she hissed. "What if he discovers the truth?"

"Playing by the rules never got me anywhere," Blackthorn said, watching the streets, which were just beginning to come alive with carriages, pedestrians, and vendors selling goods.

Several minutes later, the guard returned and opened the door. "Follow me," he said. "I suggest staying close or I can't guarantee yer safety."

Blackthorn pulled Amelia close to him and held her

hand. She linked her fingers with his without hesitation, her warm hand soothing him. He didn't like her being here, and her insistence was beginning to concern him more than he liked. They went through another iron gate and it closed with a loud clank. He felt her jump in fright. "Just stay close and you'll be fine," he assured her with a smile.

They made a quick right and went through another metal door, then continued down the narrow hall and through a wooden door. They were instructed to sit and wait in what looked to be a warden's study.

He watched Miss Knight; she was awfully quiet. Too quiet.

"What do you plan to do if she is here?" she asked.

"Get her out."

"How will you manage that?" she asked.

"Not by force, if that's what you are thinking," he said. Prisoners died, but some did escape. "We will have to pay them."

"What if that doesn't work?" She looked at him with uncertainty.

"Let me do the talking." He would have to get a feel for the kind of man the warden was. But more often than not, money seemed to solve most problems.

Just then, the door swung open and a warden walked in. There was a shrewd look in his eyes, a look that told Blackthorn this place was starting to eat away at his soul, but Blackthorn couldn't be certain if he could be bribed.

"I hear you want to see a prisoner," he said, sitting down at his desk. The warden watched the two of them carefully, as though trying to assess who they really were. It wasn't often the prisoners had visitors here. "Do you have the documents to warrant this visit?"

There weren't any formal documents to warrant a visit. The warden wanted money. Blackthorn pulled out a sealed envelope. "Before I hand this over, I need to know if Millie Penn is in this prison"

The man's mouth twisted, and there was a spark of knowledge in those soulless eyes when he heard the name.

"No," he finally said. When he saw that Blackthorn was about to put the envelope back in his coat pocket, he quickly said, "But I know who might know where she is."

"I need to speak to her."

"By all means," the warden said, walking out of the study and directing them to follow him.

The entire time, Miss Amelia Knight was quiet and pale, which didn't surprise Blackthorn. Even the most hardened individuals feared this place. They both followed the warden out of the study and made several turns deep into the building where the prisoners were kept. Blackthorn memorized the turns, and by the time they were in the men's section of the prison, he knew where he was.

Several inmates approached the thick bars and gawked at Miss Knight, making smacking noises with their lips with obscene proposals that he knew must have bothered her, but she made no reply to any of them. Brave girl.

With a yelp, she left his side, and there she stood against an iron bar in the grip of a young prisoner, hefty in size.

"Let me out of here, or I will break 'er neck," he said.

"Easy," the warden said slowly and calmly. "Let her go."

Blackthorn slid his hand into his coat pocket and felt the hilt of a small knife. Gripping it, he watched the culprit carefully. He saw fear burning in Amelia's eyes, but she didn't scream or yell for help. She just held on to the man's arm, trying to free herself from his grip. The prick leaned in and licked her cheek and whispered something in her ear. His hand slid down her chest and cupped her breast as she bit her lip and closed her eyes in terror.

Blackthorn's training and instinct kicked in with lightning speed, as everything he'd been trained in came in full force. Before the felon could harm her, Blackthorn moved speedily and stabbed the culprit in his side through the iron bars several times with swift and precise motions. The prisoner released her, and he pulled away in agonizing pain. Just then, several guards ran to them to give assistance.

Blackthorn pulled Amelia into his embrace. He thought he heard a whimper from her. "You're all right. I have you now." She looked up at him, and as if by instinct, he kissed her forehead, relief washing over him. The prisoner could have easily chocked her to death.

She pulled away from him. "I'm all right." She gathered her unruly hair in place. "Shall we go?"

They walked together with the two guards behind them. This time, Amelia was ahead of him where he could keep his eyes on her as they walked through another iron door where the women and children were kept. He saw her gloved hand cover her mouth in shock.

Voices of all ages echoed through the cells, some asking for help, others weeping. He investigated the small cells that were no bigger than a tiny den, just big enough to stand in, and with a stench that made him gag. He was told the woman who may know Millie was in the fifth cell to his right.

The warden and the two guards waited by the iron door, allowing them some distance. Blackthorn walked with Amelia to the cell in question. The young woman was leaning on the brick wall, while another woman leaned against her with her arms wrapped around her body—she looked young and very ill.

The woman he had come to interview took one look at him and her eyes widened. "Wot are ye looking at?" she said with a spiteful tone.

"I'm here to ask you some questions," he said.

"Let me," Amelia said. She slowly approached the cell to speak with the woman. "I'm looking for a friend."

Blackthorn remained close by; he didn't want another incident.

"You?" the woman said. "Why would ye be looking fer a friend in here?"

"Do you know Millie Penn?"

The prisoner looked at her suspiciously for several seconds. "Wot do ye want with her?"

"Do you know where I can find her?"

The woman narrowed her eyes. "If ye think I'm giving away free information, ye got another think comin'."

Blackthorn handed the woman a shiny coin he retrieved from his pocket. "Is this what you want?"

She looked at it, and he knew she wanted it. This place didn't provide the prisoners with anything but porridge, if you could call it that, twice a day. No blankets. No mattress. Nothing. You had to pay for those so-called luxuries.

"Start talking," Amelia said. "Then I will give you the coin. Where is she now?"

The woman in the cell stared at the coin as if it were gold. "She said somethin' about going to see her lover."

"A lover?"

"Don't know the name, but I know she's carrying that bastard's child."

"She is with child?" Amelia whispered to herself in a defeated tone.

"He didn't want the baby," the woman said bitterly. "His high and mighty lordship kicked 'er off his property. That's how she ended up 'ere."

Blackthorn felt Amelia's grief, the unsaid words.

"Do you have any idea where she may be now?" he asked.

"I know she ain't with her father. That bastard beat her nearly to death when he found out she was with child and kicked 'er out. That is all I know," she blurted out. "The coin?"

Blackthorn tossed her the pound and pulled Amelia away from the bars. Hand in hand, they left through the iron doors. On their way out, Blackthorn handed the warden the envelope, and the iron gate slammed shut with a loud clank.

It wasn't until they reached the outside of the prison that he saw blood.

Chapter 14

AMELIA DIDN'T FEEL the pain, but the look on Lord Blackthorn's face startled her.

Clearly something was wrong.

He looked at her neck and she touched it and lifted her fingers to see blood. Not much, but blood nonetheless. That horrid man must have done it when he captured her and threatened to hurt her. Strange, she didn't feel the pain. It must be from the shock of it all.

Inside the carriage, Lord Blackthorn pulled out his handkerchief from an inside coat pocket. "Don't move," he said. Using the white cloth with his initials on it, he wiped away something on her neck.

She leaned in and a whiff of his earthy, delicious scent invaded her senses, and without thinking, she glided her hand up his warm neck, then up further to run her fingers through his hair. His gaze lifted to meet hers and he leaned in just a little. Closer. Closer again to inspect the cut. Then, he kissed her.

This kiss wasn't what she'd expected. His lips were warm and soft, everything opposite of what she saw in him. The delicious taste of his lips burst in her mouth. Slick and warm. This kiss was slow and more persuasive than she cared to admit, filling the hollow in her heart. Oh God, she'd never imagined a simple kiss could arouse such sinful thoughts in her.

Pressing tenderly against her, he gently shifted to get closer to her, and she welcomed it. Oh, if only he knew how much she liked this. Her arms slid inside his coat and felt the warmth of his body, his muscles flexing beneath her hands. She knew this man who was kissing her was tall and broad shouldered, but he was also muscled and well defined, and she was too curious for her good. For now, she didn't care. She slid her hands up to feel his hard chest against her palms as her hands explored the newfound planes of his torso.

She wanted to see him in all his naked glory. The shock of her own sinful thoughts sobered her. What was she doing? This could not continue. Then why wasn't she moving away from him? She told herself to stop. His mouth continued to explore hers as if exploring a new land, and yet there was something very protective about his kiss that made her want to melt into him.

Then, he slowly pulled away just as easily as he had kissed her.

Dizzying sensation slowly faded, and it took her a moment to find her voice. "Why did you do that?" The expression on his face made her regret what she'd said. God, if there was a way to kill an intimate moment, she just did a great job of it. But none of this was about romance; quite the opposite. This was a business transaction, she reminded herself.

"You seemed to need it," he said, his eyes still burning with need.

She raised her brow in question. He rose and pulled away the cloth that was stained with blood. Her blood.

"It looks like he dug his finger into your neck," he said. "We will need to clean it, but you will be all right."

"All right, but I don't want to return home. Not yet," she said. "I need some air, some distraction." She had only been in the prison for maybe thirty minutes at the most, yet she'd felt quite affected and suffocated in there. Seeing the children in the prison had been the hardest. Besides, the intimacy between them, and the kiss confused her, and she needed to clear her head.

"I am at your disposal until this evening."

"Will you be away this evening, then?" she said. He'd mentioned he would insist on making certain of her safety, no doubt as insurance, but perhaps he had other plans.

"The appointment will only be an hour, two at most."

"I don't understand how you plan to get into my house."

"That isn't something you need to worry about."

She narrowed her eyes. "Maybe I should." Exactly what had he done in the army?

He ignored her question. "We have some time. Why don't I show you the property and we'll get some fresh air. I think it will do us some good."

She had a feeling he needed a change of scenery too. Being in this carriage with this man, just the two of them, felt all too precarious, and left her wanting. Not a good thing, indeed.

For the next hour, they barely spoke, which was a little strange. But she needed to think, and this silence helped her. He only provided some quick answers to her questions regarding the landscape and London. Meanwhile, he rested his head and closed his eyes, sleeping. How could he sleep after a kiss like that?

The dark, ominous clouds slowly rolled in as the carriage closed in on the property. The breathtaking view reaffirmed her will to make this transaction happen. Once the carriage drove up the driveway, the horses came to a stop by the large wooden front door.

Lord Blackthorn helped her out of the carriage. Chilly air pricked her skin. She rubbed her hands on her arms to ward off the cold as she gazed up at the three-story Somersby Hall. Looking at the large dormer windows on the facade, she imagined herself in the parlor with plenty of natural light streaming into the house. The property was surrounded by green valleys and lush trees—plum trees and oaks that had a sense of peace.

The outgrowing of ivy creeping up the red brick walls reminded her of days when she had visited here. It would need trimming soon, but she may decide to keep it. Why on earth anyone would want to sell this property was beyond her, but it would be to her benefit, so she would not question it.

It was happening. Really happening. She wished Kate could be here to see this place.

She let out a long sigh of relief that was followed by hope that swelled in her heart and made her nearly choke with joy.

"It's beautiful," she whispered to herself. She looked at Lord Blackthorn, who was watching her most curiously. "What is it?" The hard look in his eyes softened, and there was a vulnerability about him that made her heart squeeze.

Her fingers twitched, begging to stroke the lovely silk of his dark hair. His loose curls danced in the wind, she saw him smile which seemed to ease her troubles. It was a wide, devilish, handsome smile, and it revealed a diagonal scar, about an inch long, that ran down his temple. She wondered where he'd procured such an injury. War, perhaps? This man made her want things, wish for things that were not possible for her. The last time she'd thought she was in love, terrible things had happened, and a good man had paid the price for her selfishness.

"What do you plan to do with this place?" he said without answering her question.

"Make it a home," she said. "For Millie and me." She watched Lord Blackthorn, who seemed deep in thought.

"Home," he said. "A good dream."

It was her dream. One that she planned to see to fruition, if it was the last thing she did. She wanted to ask him what he planned to do once they parted ways, but decided against it. The less she knew about him the better, she reminded herself again.

Millie came to mind. She would love this place. The woman in prison had said Millie was with child. Suddenly, thinking back to the night at the alley, Amelia remembered the woman she had attempted to help had been with child, and she had been angry too. Surely, she would have said something if it was Millie. Why wouldn't she?

"Perhaps later we can ride out to see the estate."

"Ride?" she said with uncertainty. "Oh, I am not sure if that is a good idea."

"Why not?" he said. "I would think some fresh air would do us some good."

"I . . . um . . ." she started. "I don't know how."

He blinked, then raised his brow. "You've never learned?"

"My grandmother didn't feel it served her purpose." She saw the curiosity in those eyes, eyes that sometimes made her want to melt into them. She'd said too much. "It is a generous offer."

"What purpose was that?" he asked.

She said nothing for a few seconds, could think of nothing to say and was afraid she had revealed too much already. He watched her intently. There was something in his eyes that made her want to share her dreams, her pain, with him.

"I was bred with one goal, to wed a man with a title and she didn't want to risk injury"

His eyes softened. "I see."

"Don't look at me like that."

He stared at her, his hard, stony features once again softening. "Like what?"

"Like some lost, pathetic woman who needs rescuing." She paused to look away at the house. "I just felt that you deserved an answer."

"Did she hurt you?"

She almost chuckled out loud. Had her grandmamma hurt her? Emotionally and physically, yes. The daily abuse had been like daily meals. On schedule. Every day.

"You can trust me," he said, as if he'd read her mind. "I will never hurt you."

His tone was filled with reassurance, and she stopped and reached out to touch his warm cheek. For several seconds, neither of them looked away. The distance between them seemed to dissolve, leaving the world behind. His gaze was soft as a gentle caress and she stood on her tiptoes to kiss his cheek. "Thank you."

"Come, it's never too late to learn to ride," he said softly. "There is nothing to it."

"It's thoughtful, but no." She watched him study her, and she knew she was not going to win this one.

"You can ride with me to get used to the animal." When she opened her mouth to protest, he quickly said, "Besides, it's a big property and you will not be able to scour the land on foot on your own."

She frowned, but something tickled in her chest. Within a few minutes of walking to the stables together, he readied the horse. It was a beautiful beast with a black flowing mane and muscles that flexed when it shifted its weight side to side.

He told her to put her foot on the stirrup and helped her up onto the beast's saddle where she held on for dear life, while he swiftly got on behind her as if he had done it all his life. He held the reins and clicked his tongue to get the horse moving. The warmth of Blackthorn's body behind her made her feel safe and secure. His large arm wrapped around her midsection and held her.

At first, they rode in a slow trot. He must have felt her discomfort because he prompted her to lean back on him. "Relax," he said softly. "I have you."

They rode on the big black stallion together, her back to the warmth of his chest. He had one hand cupping her waist while the other hand controlled the reins.

"Are you comfortable?"

"I think so," she said. The wind picked up and chilled her face. As if reading her thoughts, he shifted behind her, pulling his coat off. In one fell swoop, he put the coat on her.

"Better?" she heard him say in a low voice. The dizzying sensation of his warm coat and his intoxicating scent left her speechless.

After several minutes passed, she relaxed into him. Neither of them spoke. This kind of intimacy felt strange to her, and the warmth of him seemed to ease her tension as the hard planes of his body pressed against hers. This kind of intimacy made it all the more difficult for her to concentrate on what he was saying to her.

The green vastness was simply breathtaking. About half a mile away, she saw houses close together dotting a dirt road that went through the town. This was the town he must have been speaking about. She must take the time to visit these people once the property became hers.

"The townspeople," he said, stopping the horse on the hill overlooking the town, "they will be your tenants. There are fifteen families and you will have to look after their welfare when they seek your help. They will, in turn, provide a portion of their crops for the season." He took a deep breath, then continued as she listened. "My brother insisted on keeping the rent low and did not collect from those that were unable to pay." He paused as if he were thinking about something important. "He was a generous soul."

She sensed melancholy in his voice, but there was a touch of something else she could not define. She nearly opened her mouth to ask further about his brother but closed it. *It's none of your concern*, she thought. *The less you know of him, the better.*

"You remind me of him," he said softly.

She felt a tug in her heart. She would allow herself to feel, but at what cost? In the end, she knew nothing good could come of these feelings that were so unpredictable. The sacrifice was too great.

"You are tense," he said. "What is wrong?"

She felt his grip tighten, as if to protect her from whatever ailed her. With her back firmly against his hard chest, she was nestled between his legs. Strange tingles glided over her skin. She liked this feeling, this tenderness, but she'd never dare admit it to another soul.

"Nothing is wrong."

"I will not break your confidence."

"This place . . . it brings back a lot of memories for me."

"Oh?" he said, waiting.

"When I was a child," she started, "I used to come here and play among the ruins."

"This was your sanctuary?" His voice was warm and soothing in her ears.

"Yes, it was." She quickly chided herself for her sentimentality. No schedules. No man, or woman, for that matter, dictating how to walk, where to go, and how to behave. To breathe the air and know that she was free to choose her own path, a place to call home—*her* home.

"Is that why you want this property?" he asked.

She allowed the wind to cool her heated body. As it was, his crotch pressed hard on her buttocks when the horse swiftly climbed a low hill. "It's part of it," she said. Did her voice crack?

She felt him lean into her and he tilted her chin up with his hand to force her to look at him. Then, quite naturally, he kissed her cheek.

His soft lips lingered close to hers for a moment, and their gazes locked. His eyes were on fire, and before she knew what she was doing, their lips touched, igniting desires that soothed and frightened her at the same time. She could really fall deep the way he was looking at her.

When she tried to look away, his large hand held her chin. He reclaimed her lips, and she didn't stop him. She didn't want to stop him. The wall she had built up to protect herself slowly melted away, crumbling brick by brick. She needed to touch him. Feel him. Before her mind had grasped what she was doing, he kissed her again, tasting and exploring, and she melted into him. She wanted to feel him, all of him, and when he embraced her with his strong arms, she slid her arm up the curve of his neck.

He slowly pulled away. "I like you like this."

It took a moment for her to realize he had stopped kissing her. Still drunk with his touch and the feel of his lips on hers, she opened her eyes. For a man of his size and strength, she would have never expected how gentle he was. The flicker of fire in his eyes burned hot.

Something shifted in her. This comfort and warmth felt so good that she had lost herself in his touch. Still, she fought her emotions, because she could not afford to have these kinds of feelings for a man that she would not allow in her life.

Her cheek burned from his touch. "Why did you do that?" He'd been kissing her a lot today. This sort of intimacy must stop.

"Is it wrong to kiss my fiancée?"

"This arrangement is not permanent. It's a means to an end."

His brows quirked in amusement. "You should know, women actually enjoy my company."

"I am sure they do," she said, purposely curt.

"Just because this arrangement is temporary, it doesn't mean we can't enjoy each other."

"Just exactly what do you mean by that?"

He seemed to study her words and tone for a moment. "That isn't what I meant."

"I think I'm feeling a bit chilly. I'd like to head back to the house now if you don't mind."

"All right." With that, he steered the horse back to the stables without another word.

She had so much she wanted to ask him about the estate. And why was he kissing her and making her confused? She must give him firm boundaries; otherwise, this could easily get too complicated. After all, the only reason he was here was because of her money, and she should do well to remember that the next time he kissed her.

No, there won't be a next time, she chided herself.

When they arrived at the stables, he stepped down. He held her waist firmly and helped her down slowly, the tip of her bosom touching his chest. The intimacy between them made her warm inside. Damn his gorgeousness and that solid, towering body of his.

"Here." She pulled off the delicious-smelling coat and gave it to him.

"I'll give you a quick tour of the house, then give you time to look around on your own after."

There was a change between them, the way he kept his distance. This was good, she told herself.

Amelia followed the earl into the house. The interior of the house was better than she had imagined it. The dilapidated building had been transformed. The sweeping double staircase was simple, yet elegant.

"It's not grand, but it has its charm. My brother purchased it for his wife . . ." He paused, as if deciding if he should say more on the matter. "I must insist all the servants remain here. They have been with us for a long time and some do not have anywhere else to go. I gave them the day off to give you the freedom to roam the house. This way," he said, leading her to the stairs.

Her opinion of the earl softened when he made the comment about the servants. Day off? Her grandmother would have lashed out if any of her servants mentioned a day off. This man was proving to be a good man, which made it all the more difficult to not like him.

Amelia saw the earl's expression change, as if he were recalling a distant memory. Ah, it must be his deceased brother, but she didn't care to question him further. The less she knew about this man, the better, she told herself for the umpteenth time today. "I can see why he loved it."

"His wife that fell in love with this property."

"Where is she now?"

"She went back home to live with her parents. Why don't I give you time to look around? When you are finished here, come fetch me at the stables."

She felt a heaviness in him, so she thanked him and watched him leave. She needed to think and plan, and it was nearly impossible to do so with him near. When he strolled out of the house, she walked up the grand stairs that looked to be made of mahogany. Before her were grand paintings in the center and two smaller parallel paintings on each side. The center was a scene of a great battle, one that she wasn't familiar with. The smaller painting to her left was of a woman—young, but she carried an expression of melancholy. Below her was a painting of a young boy. To the right of the center painting was a picture of a man, quite handsome and with very similar features to Lord Blackthorn. Was he his brother? Her grandmother had given her all the information about the men on the list she was to choose a husband from and their brief histories. She knew Blackthorn had lost many family members while he was out of the country and that his father had left him with debt.

Now, being here, she felt a connection to the earl that made her want to reach out and soothe his suffering. Shaking off the senseless thoughts, she focused on the task at hand. Looking around the grand house, she walked up the stairs.

It took about an hour to walk through the house. She couldn't help but wonder why he would want to sell this place. There were two master bedrooms, four large guest rooms, and a private family parlor. Servants' quarters were on the top floor, which she didn't enter.

One could have surmised that the owner had taken pride in designing the house. The details were beautiful, with an ornate cornice above the decorative frieze in each room. A Greek-inspired marble mantel framed the hearth in the parlor on the ground floor. She looked up and saw the Rococo ceiling with baby blue and white birds and angels dancing about, and the chandelier swooped downward like a waterfall.

Her chest squeezed. Soon, very soon, all this would be hers. With quiet calm, as if the sea had settled after a storm, she walked out of the house and to the stables where Blackthorn was waiting for her.

There, she saw him with the beautiful black stallion. His coat was off and hung on the tip of a rake. His sleeves were rolled up several inches. His hands were gentle on the stallion as he brushed him, murmuring something all the while to the beast.

"Did you get to look around a bit?" he asked without looking at her.

"I did," she said. "I didn't have a chance to thank you for the flowers you sent."

"I hope I have sufficiently convinced Mrs. Pots."

So, the gesture had merely been to convince her chaperone of his affection for Amelia. "Of course," she said soberly. "I fear she is too clever. She watches me like prey every minute of the day and reports back to my grandmother."

"Then I shall have to endeavor to make certain she has no doubt in her mind about us." He turned to put the brush away and walked to her. "Shall we practice?" he said with a lift of his brow. He took her hand and kissed it. "So there isn't a doubt in her mind."

Her breath caught. Damn, those seductive eyes. She allowed his lips to linger longer than necessary. Her gaze lowered, but not before she saw him looking at her. His gaze boldly raked over her lips, her neck, and down to her bosom. Her heart quickened, racing more by the minute. Then, before she knew what was happening, he pulled back.

The dark clouds had rolled in fast, and the loud thunder seemed to be getting close. She needed to head back to town if she was going to beat the rain. But she feared that it may be too late.

"Storm is coming," he said, clearing his throat. He looked up. "Shall we go inside?"

All her life, no one had done anything purely for her consideration. He had managed it twice. Not even her own family would have done that. Could this man be any more perfect? If he had any faults, she couldn't see them at the moment. If there were such a man, he'd fit that profile without error.

She watched him roll his sleeves down and pull his coat back on. They walked quietly back to the house, and she welcomed the silence. Once ensconced, he led her to the parlor and started a fire.

"How many servants are there?" she said, trying to shift the focus away from them.

"There is a butler and a housekeeper, two footmen, two maids, a cook, and a scullery maid. The groundskeeper lives in a small cottage near the stables. The stable hand is his son-in-law." He added, looking at his surrounding, "As you can tell, it's minimally furnished, as my brother and his wife didn't get to finish decorating it after rebuilding the house."

He must miss his brother. Her grandmother had informed her before departing for London that his brother Max had always been fragile from birth, but she'd never spoken of his wife. Not that it was any of Amelia's concern, but that didn't mean she couldn't be sympathetic. "I am sorry about your brother."

His gaze rose and met hers, softening with a faint smile. The thunder rumbled outside. "The storm," he whispered, looking out the window.

"Yes," was all she could muster. Judging by the dark clouds, she was going to be stuck with this man, she thought with conflicting emotions.

"I don't think we will be getting back home anytime soon."

Chapter 15

THEY WERE BOTH ensconced in the parlor that faced the driveway.

Amelia was quiet, too quiet.

Blackthorn walked over to the fireplace and jabbed at the logs with an iron poker, then watched the growing flames. He felt her gaze on him. Oh, yes, he felt it all right.

He looked over his shoulder and saw her sitting, shoulders slumped, on the dark green settee. Suddenly, he found himself rushing to get the fire going for her. "It'll get warm soon enough," he said, walking over to her. He pulled off his coat and wrapped her in it.

"Thank you."

Years of spying had taught him to pay attention to details. What was she not telling him? Or was he reading too much into this? Was this the permanent consequence of spying for nearly a decade? To never truly trust anyone?

"What's the matter?" she said suspiciously.

"Why do you ask?"

"You look at me as though I were prey to be devoured."

He chuckled. "A hard habit to break. My occupation didn't allow me the comfort of allowing my guard down. It's been years since I've been home."

"From the war?" she said, interest in her eyes.

"Yes and no." He turned away. He didn't want to talk about spying or the dehumanizing part of his former profession with this woman, or anyone for that matter. He needed to change the subject quickly. "There is something I need to warn you about."

"Oh?" she said, frowning and pulling the coat close to her as if to ward off the cold.

The start of this morning had been bad enough with his mother back in London, ordering his servants about frantically as if she were the Queen of England. Then she had congratulated him on the engagement and how much Amelia's inheritance would mean for them. What she had meant was how much she would enjoy spending the money.

He intended to put her on a budget so that she didn't squander the entire inheritance. He may not care to be the earl, but that didn't mean he wanted to hand over a ruin to the next in line either. He was not his father and didn't plan to burden the next in line with the worries of debt.

"My mother may approach you, to befriend you." He knew his mother would corner Amelia eventually, but he didn't want her to be frightened of his conniving mother. Better that he be with her most of the days to come until they would go their separate ways. "I insist you keep your distance from her."

"If you like, I will do as you wish," she said. "But do you mind telling me why?"

His mouth thinned. He didn't want to get into this, but she did deserve to know at least what she was getting herself into. What was he going to say? Giving it some thought, he said, "Let's just say she has ulterior motives, and more often than not, they involve her own selfish schemes. Do not promise her anything or agree to anything until you discuss it with me first."

Her brows pulled together in confusion. "I will," she said.

There was a question in her tone, but he ignored it. If something happened to her, his own plans to leave this damn place may take longer than necessary. Meanwhile, he'd do his best to keep his investment safe for their own good, even from his mother.

He watched her quizzical expression. God, there was this innocence beyond her determined exterior. He wanted to peel away those layers and see what was beneath them. He could not deny the struggle he sensed in her. And at times, when she didn't know he was looking, he noticed her deep in thought and a sense of loneliness there too. He had a talent for reading people. That was one of the reasons the Home Secretary had recruited him—that and his talent for breaking codes.

He'd suffered brutal weather, lack of sleep, and physical pain while training. But being here at his brother's estate with so many memories, brought back feelings he'd buried for so long. Too many sorrows and deaths in Somersby Hall.

He was glad Amelia would make it her own. It was time

this house was filled with new memories, and perhaps Miss Knight would do just that. There was a part of him that wanted to hold her in his arms and ease whatever troubled her. Riding together didn't help sate his need to be near her, to soothe her troubles. Or to ease his own loneliness, the lust he sometimes felt for her. Either way, he knew he was walking a thin line in this matter.

Shaking his head, he inhaled and pushed those thoughts away. Whatever his troubles were, he didn't have the luxury of indulging in them. Or her. The thunder and rain outside broke his train of thought. "I'm getting hungry," he said. "Let's get something to eat, shall we?"

Did he expect her to cook for him? The only thing she knew how to do in a kitchen was slice the bread. "The servants aren't here." She watched his expression to see his reaction.

"I may not know much about the kitchen, but I can find us something to eat. I even taught myself how to make a meal or two."

"In the army?" she asked, surprised by his admission.

He nodded, as if he were proud of himself for saying such a thing. An earl would never admit this to his peers, but then again, she wasn't really his peer, was she? Not really. Just a lowborn woman who now had the means to gain her independence.

She watched him with curiosity as he moved about the kitchen. This man was something of an enigma. He fought with prisoners, bribed wardens, and sneaked into homes without getting noticed. Was there anything he couldn't do?

She recalled the way his gentle hands had soothed

her, the way he'd protected her in prison. She had been bombarded with the sight of the children and woman in the cells, knowing full well Millie could easily be one of them. Her heart had reached out to them, but in the end, she could not help any of the women and children in there.

He took her hand in his, his warm, calloused hand wrapping around hers like a thick blanket, and led her through the servants' stairs and down to the kitchen below the ground floor. After spending the day together, his touch was becoming natural to her.

She liked this quiet affection, this physical attraction or whatever one called it. She didn't even know what it was. They were engaged, only as a means to an end. Once they both got what they wanted, they would go their separate ways. That was a certainty.

So why not enjoy him while they were in each other's company? What harm would it do? It was better than bickering with this man. Besides, it would do them good to convince the world they were well suited.

Once ensconced in the kitchen, she looked around the quiet room. It was large, and in the middle of it there was a large wooden table. She sat on a stool and watched him. There was a tall, large dresser with plates, pots, and pans. He seemed to be searching for something as he checked baskets and cabinets. Then he disappeared down the hallway.

"Where are you going?" she said as he disappeared.

No more than five minutes later, he returned with a bottle of wine and a loaf of bread in his hand. Setting it aside on the wooden table, he found a knife, two glasses, and two plates from the dresser and started slicing the bread. Then he grabbed the butter that was on the counter and slathered it on the bread and handed it to her. She was amused, and quite enjoyed watching him go about the kitchen. As it was, she had a difficult time not staring at him like a love-sick girl.

She took the first bite and closed her eyes as the butter melted in her mouth. Creamy and delicious. The bread was thick and soft in the center and smelled fresh, as if it had been made this morning. She watched him pour wine in the glasses for them. She took a drink to wash down the bread.

"Do you really intend to stay with me in my room?" she asked. The day was growing late and the inevitable would come. He couldn't possibly think to stay in her own room.

He took a bite of the buttered bread and gulped down the wine. "Yes." Then he poured himself another.

"Honestly, I think you are overreacting," she said.

"This individual who threatened you knows where you reside and knows your name." His eyes narrowed. "We cannot risk your safety."

Until you get your money? Is that it? "Do you really think Millie could be linked to this man?" She knew the answer before she finished asking the question. "She must be so frightened."

"We can't assume she is innocent in all this," he said, drinking his wine.

She recalled that night in the alley. "Remember the girl? The woman in the prison said Millie was with child, and the girl in the alley was in the same condition. Do you think she could have been Millie? What are the chances?"

"Why is it so important for you to find this woman?"

"I made a promise."

"Promises are often broken."

"Not by me."

Just when she thought he would argue with her, he did something quite surprising. He leaned in and kissed her on the mouth. His warm lips had a tinge of the taste of wine and butter, soft and delicious. She kissed him back, quite unexpectedly, as if it were the most natural thing to do. And just as easily as he kissed her, he pulled away.

"Why did you do that?"

He pointed to the corner of her lips. "Butter," he said. "Besides, you seem to enjoy it when I kiss you."

She wiped it off with her finger. "I do not." She smiled. "Maybe a little."

Just then his eyes became sharp and focused. "I need you to tell me the names of people your friend may seek out or know."

"There are only two people I can think of. Cook and her papa. I have an inkling where Cook may be. Millie's father rented a room near the pub. I don't know if he is still there. I know the prisoner said she isn't with her father, but we should make a visit to him."

"I agree," he said. "Then I'll have a visit with this Cook."

"I am coming with you."

"No, you are not."

"Yes, I—"

Before she finished her sentence, he leaned in and kissed her again.

Her lips were velvety and sweet. Oh, how he could get used to this. She was like a missing puzzle piece that fit the hollows of his empty heart, and his cock was hard with wanting. He wanted to touch her, feel every arc and bend of her soft curves and lick the peaks of her nipples until she moaned wildly in his ear. He wanted to make love to her until she fell limp in his arms with joy.

But he knew all too well that these kinds of emotions were unreliable, unpredictable, and often didn't end well. No doubt she wished him to stay, but he had no intention of staying in London for anyone, and that meant he'd have to let her go. And he would let her go because it was the only choice he had.

He pulled away. Looking into her dreamy eyes, he chided himself for kissing her.

What the devil are you doing?

Chapter 16

"WHAT ARE YOU planning?" Kendall said to himself, watching Somersby Hall from the nearby town. The rain had finally stopped as he was sitting in the carriage watching the damn property. His sources had said she was in there with the earl, and that they were up to something. What that something was, he still hadn't discovered. His sources had also told him that she'd visited the prison too. So she wasn't taking his warning seriously, was she?

Irritatingly not.

He was taking a risk in coming here, but luckily, he'd taken an extra precaution by hiring an unmarked carriage.

Amelia Knight. That damn, bloody hell name was like salt in the wound. Hell, he'd thought he was rid of that damn family. He was sorry he'd ever taken pity on her mother.

The girl he had known was all grown up. The slim curves were where they ought to be. The girl had tried to attack him that night when he'd been with her mother, that bitch. Just as her mother had been a pain in the arse after she did away with her daughter. She had packed up and disappeared the next night when he'd come for her.

The landlord had told him she hadn't mentioned where she was going, nor if she planned on coming back. Oh, how he'd been angry after that. She'd been his favorite, that much he would admit to, but his benevolence had been paid back to him with betrayal.

He had looked for her for nearly a month. Not because she'd had any meaning to him in his life, but he'd given her an expensive jewel he'd acquired at his gambling hall before calling on her. A one-karat sapphire ring, one that reminded him of her eyes. He'd thought he saw her at Hyde Park a few years back. That kind of beauty—she was a whore, but a beauty—was hard to miss. She'd been with a man and a little boy who looked to be no more than five. She'd gotten into a carriage with the man and the boy and they had driven off.

He'd never done anything like that, given a pricy jewel to a whore, but he'd been drunk and out of his mind, apparently. And now her daughter was back in town, as an heiress no less.

When he had heard some woman, a stranger, had been looking for Millie, he hadn't thought much of it, until his sources told him who this individual was.

Damn it. He did not need this trouble now. He'd planned on washing his hands of this business since his son would soon wed Lucinda. He'd wanted this for his son, a life that he'd dreamt of since he'd been old enough to remember.

Stealing his way in the streets and saving every penny of that money until he had enough to own his own pub.

From where he sat, he could see the dark clouds dispersing, and the rain had stopped. He needed to go before he risked too much.

After Kendall returned from White's, a club he frequented at St. James's Street, he entered his townhouse and quietly shut the door. When his butler arrived several minutes later and took his coat, Kendall said, "Whisky." The butler was always late in attending to his duties. He reminded himself to get rid of the old man once the Season ended.

"Right away, sir," the butler said, then walked off to get the drink.

Kendall made his way to his study and lit the candles. Once he was alone and no one was there to watch his every move, he yanked his cravat loose and untied it before tossing it on his leather chair. He did the same for his greatcoat. Sinking deep into his leather chair, he lay back, closed his eyes, and released a long sigh.

Amelia—damn girl. Why did she have to show up now, and why the hell was she looking for Millie? He'd last seen Amelia while he'd been in the middle of tupping her mother. Her mother had been a very good whore, he reflected with a smile that soon turned into a grimace.

There was a knock at the door, and he opened his eyes. He looked at the small, ornate clock on his desk. It was nearly seven in the evening.

Knock, knock.

Philip peeped in. "Father?" Philip said, watching his father's expression. "Is anything wrong?"

"Aren't you supposed to be at a dinner party?" Kendall said, trying his best to hide his annoyance.

The butler knocked, and when Kendall gave permission to enter, he walked in and placed a glass of whisky from his silver tray on the desk.

"Anything else, sir?" the expressionless butler said in a stately manner.

Kendall waved him away and the butler promptly left.

"The dinner is not until eight, Father," Philip said. He watched his father carefully.

Kendall looked at the small clock on his desk. "It seemed late. Don't you have something to do?"

"I heard you come in and wanted to see you," he said. "You look unwell, Father."

"No need to worry yourself, boy." Kendall cleared his throat again. "I had some business matters that I needed to deal with." He forced a smile, watching his son waiting for his approval.

"Of course," Philip said as if waiting for Kendall to say more. When he didn't, his son left him alone. "I've purchased the ring as you suggested, Father."

The ring for the woman he intended to propose to. The boy always needed too much encouragement to get things done. Must Kendall think of everything? It was exhausting. "Good."

"Do you want to see it?"

"Maybe later," he said. When he said nothing else to his son, Philip took the hint and left him alone. No more than a few minutes after his son had left, Mrs. Pots entered the room. "You kept me waiting a long time," she said, walking over to Kendall.

"That could not be helped. What have you discovered?" he asked. The night of the ball, he had found Amelia's chaperone drinking champagne in the corner outside the ballroom, mumbling something about how Amelia the spoiled brat had ruined her life. He had made it his business to pay attention. He had approached her, finding common ground in his opinion of Amelia Knight. With a little wooing, she had been under his thumb. This woman was starving for attention.

"Nothing yet."

Kendall had told her enough but hadn't mentioned Millie. "Try to find out, darling," Kendall said.

"I'd have more freedom if it wasn't for that Kate."

"Ah, the American woman."

"Yes," she said.

He'd seen the beautiful American friend of Amelia's. "Tell me," he said, "had Blackthorn ever called on her before the announcement?"

"No," she answered. "Why?"

"It just seems odd to me that there had been no connection between them and suddenly the engagement." He had Millie locked up, but insurance was always a good idea. Knowing the most he could about Amelia gave him the upper hand.

"It was her grandmother's wish for her to marry for title. God knows she was bred for it since Amelia arrived ten years ago, showering her with dresses and jewels."

He gave her a sideward glance. Clearly, she had issues with Amelia. None of which was his concern. "I would think there would be some form of courting before she made her decision."

"Her grandmother was very insistent she make her choice quickly, so that might have something to do with it."

"Well, keep an eye on her and see what you can find out." He faced her and turned her around. Slowly, he lifted her skirt and pulled his breeches down. Thrusting into her, he moved in and out slowly at first, then faster and faster as she moaned . . .

Chapter 17

BLACKTHORN SAT ON his chair in his study and rested his elbows on his desk, the ledger book open as he went over the accounts. He went line by line to check for accuracy, then added the cost of the flowers he'd had delivered to Miss Knight on the last line before closing it with a wide smile.

God, she drove him mad with this unrelenting need, something he had never quite experienced before. This wasn't just about lust; it was more than that, something that wasn't familiar to him.

Leaning back in his leather chair, he recalled the kiss at Somersby Hall. One that kept popping up in his mind as he sat here trying to work. He had been trained in Systema, a Russian hand-to-hand combat, and trained to endure interrogation and spy on his enemy, but with this woman, none of these were useful. But deep in the recesses of what was left of his heart, he enjoyed her company more than he liked.

There was a knock at the door, and Blackthorn gave permission to enter. Kane Roberts strolled in, donning a gray coat that reached to below his knees.

Roberts quickly took a seat in front of Blackthorn. "How's domestic life treating you?"

"I'll let you know." Blackthorn grinned. He trusted Roberts as much as a former spy can trust anyone. They'd known each other for years.

"So, why am I here?" Roberts asked the earl.

Blackthorn gave him a brief account of his involvement with Miss Amelia Knight and what had transpired in the last several days.

"I see," Roberts said. "I thought you'd finally changed your mind about leaving London and decided to submit to your duties as the new Earl Blackthorn."

"I don't want to be here any longer than I have to," Blackthorn told him. "I need you to check with the coroner to see if they've discovered a female body recently. Between fifteen and twenty years old. She's with child, so that should help in narrowing down the search."

The last kiss was still on her mind, firmly seared there by Lord Blackthorn before he took her home. Ensconced in her room with Kate, she recalled their kiss again.

Her earl. His lips were warm and inviting, his touch soft and gentle. He ignited this urge, this primal need that was so strong, it excited her to no end. How could she have been so wrong about him? She had thought he hated her.

She had thought he wanted nothing to do with her, but his kisses and touch said otherwise. "Amelia?" Kate said. "Are you listening to anything I have said?" She put down her saucer and cup on the low table in front of them.

"I'm sorry. What were you saying?" Amelia said.

"I asked you when Lord Buckthorn plans to arrive."

Amelia had informed her of the events thus far. While Amelia didn't agree that Blackthorn should be in her room, she could very well leave that vital information out and not tell Kate. "He didn't say."

"How does he plan to get into the house?"

"I don't know."

Kate sighed. "If Mrs. Pots sees him here, there will be much to pay. I suggest you lock your doors."

"I believe she has the key to the door."

"Well then, I shall have to make sure she misplaces it."

Amelia gave her a sideward glance. "Thank you. Where is she anyway? I did not see her for dinner today, not that I am complaining."

"Mrs. Pots came home a few minutes before Lord Blackthorn drove you home. She gave me a snide remark and told me she had a headache and would be retiring early today."

"Perhaps she took heed of my orders."

"What orders?"

"I told her now that I am engaged to Lord Blackthorn, I will not need a chaperone."

Kate's eyes widened. "Finally, you are speaking up for yourself. Good for you."

Chapter 18

WHERE WAS LORD Blackthorn?

He'd said he'd come tonight. Even if he only came here to safeguard his "investment" as he called it, this night made her all the more uneasy and excited.

Anxious was a more fitting word.

Kate had left the room over an hour ago, and here Amelia was standing in front of the large mirror, frowning at her blond hair that hung loose about her shoulders and her dull brown eyes. Dull, dull, dull. And her body! She didn't have voluptuous curves or a large bosom that men seemed to like and stare at. Her bosom was average, she supposed.

And she had these small freckles despite the fact that she spent most of her days indoors. She touched her lips that were too full—

No, no, no. What was she doing? Why on earth was she doing this to herself, staring at her body and face as if she were to be presented to a man on a platter? And why now?

She had never looked at herself this way before. She was acting like a harlot waiting to hook a customer, and that notion made her ill.

She groaned and slowly walked over to her bed and slipped under the thick blanket. Should she have blown out the candles? Or left them burning for him? Oh, heavens, this man was driving her mad. There was really no need for him to come and stay in her room. It was scandalous. She looked at the window that had been fixed since this afternoon.

Honestly, Amelia, she said to herself. *He may not even come.* Then, slow creaks on the floor got her attention. She jerked up, looking around the room, her heart pumping hard in her chest. She listened in the dark for several seconds, but there was nothing. No Lord Blackthorn. Perhaps he had changed his mind. Quite unlike him. He seemed like a man who kept his promises.

She shook it off and lay back down. Less than ten minutes later, she was drowsily falling asleep. In her dream, Lord Blackthorn came to her, kissed her goodnight and sat on the chair near the hearth to watch her sleep. She felt protected. Loved.

Lovely dream indeed . . .

Then she heard someone talking. She tried to open her eyes, but her eyelids were heavy. Rubbing them, she tried to open her eyes again. When she did, the room was dark. Had the candlelight gone out? It must have.

"I had no choice," someone mumbled in the dark.

She held the blanket close to her. Someone was in her room. "Who's there?" she said. Nothing for several seconds.

"Should have been there . . ." came the voice again.

"Hello?" She quickly lit the candles next to her. As the room slowly came to light in a warm yellow hue, she saw *him*.

On her chair next to the hearth, Lord Blackthorn sat sleeping in a most uncomfortable position, his coat half falling off him, his long legs stretched out in front of him. When had he arrived? Her heart leaped for joy that he had come, but the fact that he could sneak into and out of her house did not give her comfort.

She got up and walked over to him and watched him for a minute. She reached out to touch the dark strands of his hair, but stopped. Afraid to wake him, she allowed herself to enjoy the intimacy of this moment. The stubble was coming in dark now and she had an urge to touch it. Rather than fulfil her wants, she let her gaze trail lower to his lips with a tugging in her heart. She tasted them. Caressed them with her own mouth.

"No, stop this. Someone will get killed," he mumbled.

She knelt next to him and watched him. His brows creased with worry and a muscle quivered at his jaw as if he were in pain.

"Lord Blackthorn," she said softly, shaking him gently at first, then giving him a shove to get him to open his eyes. In one swift motion, he had a knife to the base of her neck. His eyes were intense, black and ready to attack.

She dared not move. It took a moment for Lord Blackthorn to realize who she was and what he had done. He put the knife down and sat up. He took a moment to compose himself.

"What happened?" he said, running his hand through the thick of his hair.

She touched her neck. "You had a nightmare."

"I'm sorry about the knife." He tucked it inside his boot. "A habit hard to break."

She stood up and sat on the edge of her bed. "It's all right. You didn't know." She watched him stand and wipe his face with his hands. "When did you arrive?" The candlelight splashed across him, giving sharp contrast to the contours of his handsome face.

He looked at the small mantel clock. "About an hour ago."

"Why did you not wake me?" she asked.

"You were sound asleep." He smiled. "Go back to sleep."

All of a sudden, she felt naked as his eyes raked over her, then slowly dropped to her bosom. "So you can watch me all night?"

He walked over to her and she stood to meet his eyes, her back against the bedpost.

"I will not watch you. Go to sleep," he whispered with a smile, and kissed her forehead, but he didn't touch her with his hands. "Sleep, my sweet Amelia."

The sound of her name on his lips was like candy. She wanted to hear it again and again. "Does this mean I can call you Richard?"

"Yes," he answered. "In fact, I prefer it."

God, why did he have to smile like that? There was a warmth that echoed in his voice, one that made her heart melt with need. This strange need that had kept tugging at her all day today. This need that she could no longer deny.

"I insist we share the bed."

"No," he said, watching her.

Well, at least she knew he had no interest in her that way. Why did this not surprise her? What would a man like him, an earl, gain from her other than the inheritance? Was that all she was worth? Her money? She turned to walk away, and he stopped her, pulling her close to him.

"I want to," he confessed, "but I can't."

"Why not?" she said. That didn't help either. "It's just a bed, Richard." She watched as his gaze fell to her lips.

"Believe me, you don't want me in that bed," he whispered. He lifted her chin. "I can't promise that I will behave if I am in that bed with you."

"Then don't," she said, shocked that she had actually said it. Her heart pumped wildly in her chest at the prospect of making love to this man, to be bound naked together, to feel the warmth of his manhood inside her. She had fought it, and she couldn't fight it any longer. She wanted him, wanted to taste him just this once. She might as well, knowing that the rest of her life would be spent without men.

"I can't, knowing what I will do and I will have to leave you," he confessed. "Believe me when I say that I don't intend to remain married to you or stay in London. I can't give you that."

"I know," she said, searching his eyes. "I don't expect this to be more than what is it." She was her mom's daughter, she thought with irony. But if that was the case, why fight it tonight, when she had a gorgeous man standing in front of her?

"What do you think this is?" he asked.

"Lust."

His brows lifted. "Oh, my sweet, it's far more than that."

This was entirely dangerous, but she knew if she didn't do it now, she'd lose her nerve. Even now, her body ached for his touch. She lifted her chin and on tiptoe, kissed him on his warm lips. It was more like a peck, and he made no move to kiss her back.

"Think of it as a favor," she whispered to him. "Take off your clothes." She stepped away. "I want to see you. All of you." This was not like her. Not even close, but it was intensely liberating.

He said nothing. Oh, the anticipation was too great, too delicious. She sat down on the chair and watched him, rippling with excitement.

He loosened his cravat and tossed it aside, and her heart leaped. Then he pulled his shirt off in one swift motion and tossed it on the floor. "Is this what you want to see?"

She gulped at the beauty before her. Oh, yes. The planes of his chest were as flat as a board, with ripples of muscles on his midsection, and above the gold beauty of his stomach, his chest swelled with muscles. Muscles that flexed as he moved his arms, all the while not looking away from her.

Her eyes raked from his powerful shoulders down to his muscled arms—arms that now removed his boots, one by one, tossing them aside. Then his hand fiddled with the button to remove the breeches and he quickly tossed them. In that instant, when he faced her in the dimness of candlelight, her breath caught, and for several seconds she forgot to breathe.

His manhood was erect and proud as he walked closer to her. Speckles of black curls at the base of him made her want to reach out and touch them, unable to look away. God, he was glorious. Beautiful.

He took her hand in his and helped her cup his erection and slowly stroke it. He was warm and soft. Very soft. She felt the agonizing ache between her legs and her nipples perked up painfully.

Looking up, she saw the fiery intensity in his eyes, and she knew he was enjoying this. So was she, sinfully so.

"This isn't fair," he let out between hot breaths. "I want to see you."

"In a moment," she breathed out, enjoying the feel of him in her hand. Then just as naturally, she licked the tip of his erection with her tongue, tasting his heated flesh that felt like velvet in her mouth. The flavor of him was foreign to her, but she knew she liked this. More than liked it, actually.

"Let me," he groaned out.

She stopped kissing him there. He gave it a few more strokes as she watched him in delight. With a final tug, he released his seed into the cravat he'd picked up from the floor.

He pulled her up to meet him and slowly pulled her gown over her head and tossed it, moving his lips down her neck to the erect mounds of her nipples. She gasped at the sensation when he licked her nipple with his tongue, as if he could not satisfy his hunger.

This delightful touch was like being in paradise, and

she didn't want it to end. She ran her fingers though his black hair. He moved lower, but he didn't stop licking and kissing her. Then, he lifted her in his arms and took her to bed. He nestled himself next to her and kissed her again.

"My turn to please you."

"You already did," she said, searching his eyes.

"Believe me, my sweet, you will enjoy this." He kissed his way down.

"What are you doing?"

"Pleasing you," he said, meeting her eyes and smiling. "Let me."

He kissed her belly, then moved lower, kissing her all the way to the apex of her sex. He kissed her gently, and she widened her legs for him. She was wet and throbbing for him. This ache was unbearable. Just then, as if he heard her plea, he licked deep into her heat, sucking as she moaned in pleasure. Oh God, what was he doing to her? This sensation was more than she could bear, and his tongue was doing magical things to her as he licked the valley of her sex until her core throbbed, and she climaxed.

He came up to join her and kissed her forehead. "Sleep, my sweet." He pulled the blanket over them and pulled her close to him, her buttocks pressing hard on his erection. His arms embraced her. "We have a long day tomorrow."

"Richard," she whispered. "What were you dreaming about?"

He was quiet for a moment. "Max."

"Your brother?"

"Yes."

She wondered what he'd been through that would cause nightmares. She waited a few minutes before asking him, but before she could speak, she heard a soft snore as he quickly fell asleep. She smiled. This feeling, this warmth next to him, felt so right. She felt so comforted and protected. When she pulled away to put out the candle on the candelabra, he pulled her back to him.

"Where are you going?"

"Putting out the candles so we can sleep." She blew the flame out then snuggled into him again. He wrapped his arms around her, and she soon fell asleep.

It wasn't until several hours later that Blackthorn awoke in the darkness in her room and felt the soft curves of Amelia next to him. This beauty that was curled up to him and sound asleep, his angel.

He sighed, knowing this could not last and he could not give her what she would ultimately want from him. Nothing in this world, not even this beauty next to him, would change his mind on that fact.

Gently removing himself from the bed, he put on his shirt, breeches, and boots. Putting his arms into his coat, he slipped out of the room as easily as he had come in and faced the cool early morning of London.

Just before sunrise, he thought, as he closed the door that led to the mews. He'd go home, get changed, and eat breakfast before they looked for Cook. Pulling his collar up to ward off the morning chill, he briskly walked toward his townhouse.

Chapter 19

"WHAT ARE YOU doing here?" Blackthorn said, holding back his anger. He'd just finished his breakfast in his study when he'd heard the commotion in the foyer and went to investigate the ruckus. His mother's footman was bringing in her bags and belongings, with her maid trailing behind her.

"I'm here to help with the wedding, of course," his mother said. "You don't expect me to not be involved, do you?"

"We agreed you would stay in Blackthorn Hall."

"No, dear boy. I never agreed to anything."

"My God, how many servants do you lug around with you?"

"As many as I need," she said. "Now, take those up to my room, dear girl. Tell the housekeeper I will have a menu ready for her tonight."

"There won't be a grand wedding. I am acquiring a special license to marry in the privacy of my home. Then we're off to Scotland to meet her grandmother."

His mother's mouth opened as if to argue with him. "Is this what she wants?"

"Yes, we both agreed on this."

"But she is an heiress. Her family will not want this."

"Her grandmother wants a quick wedding, believe me in this."

She narrowed her eyes. "Is she with child?"

"Not that it's any of your concern, but no."

"This woman cannot know what she is missing. She must have a grand wedding. I have already informed my friends and family members of this grand news."

"You'll just have to un-inform them."

"I will do no such thing. Do you know the scandal this will cause?" She paced the room. "I must speak to your fiancée."

"No." He stepped up to his mother. "You will not speak to her. Or approach her without my permission," he said with sudden protectiveness.

"Don't speak to me with that tone. I am still your mother."

"My mother?" he said. "Yes, you are. Tell me, where were you when Max died, and when he was asking for you after you left us? When Father asked for you to come to Max's funeral? Where were you when Father died?"

"I . . . I . . ." she said in a bereaved tone. "I wanted to come, but you know how your father was. He could be cruel and heartless. You know this firsthand."

"So, you didn't come because you didn't want to face your husband?"

"You cannot know the misery that man put me through."

"Enough of this," Blackthorn said. "When I return home, I don't want you here. Now, return to Blackthorn Hall today."

He had no time to argue with his mother further. Sooner or later he would have to make her understand he had no intention of staying in London. Shaking his head, he ordered his baffled butler to assist until he came home later.

Amelia woke to an empty bed in the early morning.

Richard had slipped out in the middle of the night without waking her. While she had hoped he would stay, she told herself it was better that he'd left. It would be utterly awkward to face him in the morning. In fact, she wanted to pretend last night had never happened.

"What are your plans today?" Kate asked, sipping hot chocolate across from her in the morning room. "Will you see Lord Blackthorn?"

"Yes, I suppose so," Amelia said. She tried to avoid extensive conversation with Kate, because eventually Kate would discover what she had done with Richard, and she wasn't ready to share that experience with anyone yet.

"Hmm, an interesting answer," Kate said. "You're awfully strange this morning." Kate put her cup down on her saucer.

"I am?" Amelia said. "Where is Mrs. Pots, anyway? I haven't seen her this morning."

"Isn't that a good thing?"

"It is," she said. Perhaps the woman finally understood that Amelia really did not need her. Perhaps she didn't want to face the earl insisting that she come along on every excursion. Either way, Amelia was happy to be free of her. "Do you have plans?" She needed to take the conversation away from herself.

"Actually, I have a friend who is in town. He arrived this morning."

This was a rarity. Kate had seldom spoken of her friends or her past to Amelia before. "That's wonderful news. Perhaps we can have tea together in the afternoon."

Kate shook her head. "He is here on business and will not have much time. I am meeting him at the Grillon Hotel in an hour. He is staying only for a few days, then he will be heading up to Norfolk to see relatives."

Amelia would have liked to meet one of Kate's friends. But she knew Richard would be coming for her soon to look for Cook. Hopefully sooner than later, as she was ready to leave now.

It was nearly ten in the morning when Richard came to call. Finally, Mrs. Pots greeted the earl when she walked down the stairs, but said nothing else before she left the foyer. Good; the woman at least knew how to behave in the presence of an earl.

While Amelia grabbed her bonnet, gloves, and spencer jacket, he waited quietly in the foyer. Too quietly. From the way he stood there, it was as if nothing had transpired between them last night. This realization irked her. Irked and embarrassed her.

"You look lovely this morning," he said.

"Thank you."

He led her to the carriage parked outside.

"Where are we going?"

"We're not going anywhere."

"Then why are we in this carriage?"

"You're going to tell me everything you know about Cook; then I will inquire about this man on my own."

"Didn't we already discuss this?" She was beginning to wonder if he took her words seriously. Why was she in such a foul mood this morning, anyway? "I am going with you."

He sighed heavily. "My sweet—"

"No, please don't call me that," she barked. "I am going with you."

He observed her most curiously. "You are brusque this morning."

"So are you, might I add." She took several breaths to calm herself. "I am merely expressing my concern and if I happen to be short this morning, then so be it." She breathed in slowly. "Why is it so difficult for you to understand I need to be part of this?" This was a risk, she knew. A risk she had to take, as sooner or later he'd discover the truth about her birth, that she was the daughter of a whore. It was as if this were a real engagement, a real marriage, she thought with a stab to her heart.

"You want to know the truth?" he said with a grimace. "I can't do my job and get things accomplished when you're with me."

"Why? Because you don't care to involve me in your affairs?"

"No, bloody woman," he blurted out. "Because I fear for your safety and I need to be clearheaded in this."

"Oh," she said. "Why didn't you say so?" He didn't want baggage or to have to worry about her. Thoughtful, she thought, but still she would rather go with him. It would be lovely to see Cook again.

"Must you always fight me?" he said. When she opened her mouth to speak, he kissed her quite passionately for a long minute, reminding her of how they had been together last night. "Trust me. I will find Cook if he is in London."

"All right, I will remain home this time."

She spent about an hour telling Richard everything she knew of Cook while the carriage drove around Hyde Park. Where he worked and who he knew. She kept quiet about the more intimate stories that would reveal her past. The morsels Cook had given her when she had been hungry. How he had always made her feel safe and made her laugh. Her mother had often cried on his shoulder too, and Amelia used to wonder what had caused her so much sorrow. Richard did not need to know that. She touched the necklace her mother had given her, wondering why her mother had never written one letter, or attempted to visit her.

"Is that all of it?" Richard asked.

"Yes," she said, touching the stone on her silver necklace again.

"It's special to you."

"What is?"

"The necklace," he said. "I never see you without it."

She sighed. "I suppose it was, once. I guess it's out of habit, more than anything, that I keep putting it on every morning."

"Are you sure?"

"I am sure. I should get rid of it," she said with a pang of hurt pricking her heart. The carriage came to a stop in front of her townhouse. "We could have easily spoken in the parlor."

"I suppose, but I wanted you to myself this morning, even for a brief moment."

"Richard," she said. "About last night…"

"We'll talk later," he said, and helped her off the carriage.

It took him half a day to track down Cook. He had not been at the pub Amelia had told him about. He found Cook a mile away at another pub where he had been working in the kitchen for nearly a year. Blackthorn met with an overweight man in his fifties donning an apron.

Initially Cook had been reluctant to say anything about Millie, but when Blackthorn revealed that Amelia was his fiancée, Cook spoke without reservation. He spoke of her mother, Amelia's childhood, and Millie.

Blackthorn's heart tugged at the brutal childhood Amelia and Millie must have endured in the slums of St. Giles among the murderers and thieves. A sense of admiration pulled at his heartstrings, too. After about an hour of talking, Cook mentioned Philip.

"Philip Kendall?" Blackthorn asked. When Cook nodded, he asked, "What about him?"

"He used to come and look fer Millie 'ere. He liked her all right. I told her it wasn't a good idea, told her many times. She wouldn't listen and now look wot happened. She's with child and missing. Damn girl. I told 'er not to get herself involved with him."

This was going to get a lot more complicated with Philip involved. While he was a decent young man, he allowed his father to dictate his life. Surely his father would hate to have this information revealed to the public. Philip's father would most likely do just about anything to hide this shame.

Blackthorn thanked the man and left the pub. If he recalled, Sir Kendall had a membership at White's. While Sir Kendall spent time at the club, Blackthorn wasn't certain about Philip. Perhaps he'd go and speak with the owner. His family still had a membership there, so it wouldn't be difficult to find out.

Entering the private club, he was quickly greeted by an impeccably dressed footman.

"Will you be requiring your private room, my lord?" he asked.

"Yes," Blackthorn said. "Has Mr. Philip Kendall been here?"

"I believe Sir Kendall and Mr. Kendall arrived an hour ago," he said, looking toward a seat next to the window.

Blackthorn followed his gaze and saw one man, his back to him. "Can you inform Mr. Philip Kendall I'd like to speak to him in my private room?" he said. "Discreetly."

With that done, he walked to the back of the club where the private rooms for exclusive members were located. He ensconced himself, poured himself a scotch, and downed it in one gulp, waiting. Within five minutes, there was a knock at the door.

"Come in."

The door swung opened and Philip came in to join him. "This is a surprise," he said. "I don't often get invited to drink in such an exclusive part of the club."

These rooms were reserved for lords and persons of great influence. "It's been a long time. Sit."

Philip eagerly sat across from Blackthorn and ordered his drink from the private footman stationed outside the door. Blackthorn waited until Philip had his drink.

They exchanged pleasantries and talked about Blackthorn's recent engagement and the war. Philip shared the news of his engagement to Lady Lucinda and how pleased his father was.

"Are you pleased with the engagement?" Blackthorn asked.

Philip nodded. "She is exquisite. I am pleased, actually. Yes, I am very pleased." There was something disconcerting in his expression.

"Then why do I sense hesitation in your tone?" Blackthorn was never one to shy away from getting to the truth. In fact, he believed in getting to the point. Easier that way. "Does this have anything to do with Millie Penn?"

It was then that Philip's expression changed. "How do you know her?"

"That isn't the issue here," Blackthorn said, leaning forward to look at the young man who was now nervous. "Listen carefully, because I won't repeat what I am going to

189

tell you. Millie is with child and she is missing. If you have any information about her, I need to know."

"She is with child?"

Blackthorn watched Philip get up and pace the room, raking his hair nervously.

"How many months?"

"I don't know."

"My father cannot know this," he said anxiously. "He will murder me."

The woman in the prison had said that Millie had gone to see her lover and he had tossed her out. "So you knew nothing about this?"

Philip shook his head.

There was only one man who could have done this. Sir Kendall. The young man looked so frightened that Blackthorn decided to spare him the details and how his father may be involved in all this. It must have been Sir Kendall that kicked her out of his property when she came to see Philip. That didn't mean Sir Kendall would resort to kidnapping and murder, but self-preservation was a powerful force. Blackthorn knew this firsthand.

Perhaps the girl was in hiding. But he knew oftentimes a woman like her didn't have many places to go. The likelihood that Sir Kendall was involved in her disappearance was high.

"She loves me, and I would have married her, if not for my father," Philip said. "I am an only child and son. I cannot disappoint the man."

"Are you aware she came to see you?" Blackthorn said.

He shook his head. "No."

Blackthorn understood that, too. There was shame in his expression. This young man needed to grow a spine. "I am not telling you to confront your father," he stated. "But I need you to be aware and keep an eye open for Millie. If you hear anything, let me know."

"I will," he said. "How are you involved in this?"

"I am doing this as a favor to a friend."

Chapter 20

"Y OU HAVE ARRIVED," Amelia said, entering the parlor, where Richard sat. "Have you discovered anything?" It was nearly five in the afternoon. She'd been worried all day, and had even been tempted to drive out to Whitechapel, but hadn't since she'd told him she wouldn't.

He stood and met her halfway, embracing her and kissing the top of her head. "Hello, my sweet."

Goodness. In his warm embrace, the familiar scent of him made her forget for a moment. "Stop toying with me," she said. "Tell me, what have you discovered?"

They both sat down on the couch and he started to tell her about his day.

"I found Cook." With softness in his eyes he watched her, waiting for her reply.

"You did?" she said, ecstatic. "How is he? What did he say?"

"He is fond of you." He looked as if he wanted to tell her something more, but he didn't.

"What is it?"

"It's nothing," he said, touching her cheek. "Cook doesn't know where Millie is, but he mentioned Philip. He is Sir Kendall's only child." He paused for a few seconds before speaking again. "I think Millie is carrying his baby."

Memories of her past came rushing back. Memories of Kendall coming to see her mother and how her mother would send her to stay with Cook. How she hated that man.

"You know him?"

"I do, unfortunately," she said. "He and my mother were . . . involved. Please don't ask me any more." There was a moment of silence as she fought back conflicting emotions. "So, are we going to make a visit to Philip?"

"I already spoke to him." Richard told her of the meeting and, in the end, she felt more helpless about ever finding Millie. "He doesn't know where she is, but the child is likely his from the way he responded."

"So, after all this, we still don't know where she is?"

"Not yet; the search has just started. Give it time."

"She is with child and she may give birth soon, and in the streets." The thought made Amelia tear up. "No one deserves that."

"I have a feeling she isn't roaming the streets."

"What do you mean?"

"Is there anyone in this town that might have a grudge against you? From the past?"

"No," she said, thinking. "The only person in town who knew me as a child is—"

"Kendall?"

She nodded. "But I don't understand why he would want to hurt Millie."

"I have one more person I need to see tonight."

"Who?"

"Roberts," he said. "He may have some information that may help us."

"You will not come tonight?" she said, feeling foolish.

"Not tonight. I think it's best if I survey the neighborhood from outside."

"I see," she said. She knew she should be focused on finding Millie, but she could not help but wonder if he regretted last night. Of course he did. They had both agreed not to make this complicated. To keep their distance. It was a mistake. She was the one who had told him there would not be any physical contact between them, and now look what she'd done. Things were getting complicated. It was better if he stayed away.

Then why did she suddenly feel so uncertain and so confused?

Blackthorn arrived at Bow Street at nearly six-thirty in the evening.

The place was teeming with colorful people of all ages and both sexes. He'd been asked to wait in a room as Kane Roberts was breaking up a fight in a cell. There was a large window with faint light splashing in. He pulled out a wooden chair and sat down next to the wooden desk with piles of paper on it.

"Blackthorn," Roberts said, walking into the room and sitting down at his desk. "My apologies, but these ruffians seem to only respond to violence, rather than reason."

"I know what you mean," Blackthorn said. "What have you discovered?"

"There were multiple bodies in the last few weeks . . . young women of all sizes in the Thames," he said, "but none carrying a child."

He let out a sigh of relief. It would be more than difficult to deliver the news to Amelia if her friend were found dead.

Chapter 21

BLACKTHORN WOKE IN his bedchamber in his London townhouse to the sound of a muffled voice downstairs. Having gone to bed at four in the morning, he cursed at the ruckus downstairs.

Bright light spilled through the crack between the dark curtains. He ran his hands over his face and pulled off the counterpane.

Another shout punctuated the hall, this time sharp, as if someone were hurt. He quickly grabbed a robe, pushed his arms through the sleeves, and left his room to find out what the bloody hell was going on so early in the morning. As he stepped down the stairs, what he saw angered him.

Clark, his butler, had a girl by the arm and was subjecting her to the humiliation of being treated no better than a gutter rat.

"Release her."

The young woman jerked away from the butler when he released her and looked up at Blackthorn. She had on a tattered dress in a dull, light gray color with an apron still tied tightly around her waist as if she had been preparing a meal. Her hair looked as though it hadn't been washed in weeks, and she looked as if she hadn't slept in days.

Blackthorn walked up to Clark. "Take the girl to the parlor and get her something to eat while I get dressed."

Clark had the audacity to give him an infuriated look before he escorted the girl. Damn butler. Blackthorn quickly noted that he needed to speak with his staff about how one treats another human being, despite their station. Granted, he'd been gone most of the years he had owned the townhouse, spying for former Home Secretary Tomkin, but he didn't think he'd need to remind the staff who the boss was in his own house.

He quickly changed with the help of his valet and walked into the parlor. The girl was sitting on the edge of the couch nibbling on a scone, looking very distraught and out of place.

When the girl saw him, she stood and bowed to him quite awkwardly, as if she wasn't certain what she was supposed to do in his presence.

"Who are you and why have you sought me out?"

She approached him slowly and handed him a calling card. "Ye gave this to my mum, sir. She said ye will know what to do."

He took the card from her and recalled that night. It was the same card he'd given to the woman and six girls his brother had been providing for.

"What is your name?"

"Beatrice Bell, sir," she said, distraught. "Mum spoke of you. She says you were kind to her."

"Is everything all right?"

"No, sir," she said, choking with emotion. "Mum has been sick for days with fever. I didn't know where to turn, sir." Tears fell down her cheeks, and she wiped them with her hand.

Why hadn't they called a physician to see to her needs? He'd given her enough funds to live comfortably for several months.

"Will you help us, sir?"

"Wait here," Blackthorn said. He quickly gave his orders to Clark to have the driver ready the carriage. Once that was accomplished, he had the footman deliver a message to his family doctor to meet him at the address he had provided.

As he escorted Beatrice to her home, the girl kept sobbing. She could not be more than fifteen, yet there was a sense of melancholy about her, a sense of hardship on her face, one that a fifteen-year-old girl should never have to endure. But the reality was quite different. Sympathy pulled in his chest. What possible future could there be for a girl like her? Yet he told himself again and again that it wasn't his duty. He was simply assisting a woman who was ill so that she may continue to care for her girls.

"She will be all right," he assured Beatrice. He knew very well he could not promise her such things, but he felt it needed to be said.

Her smile was faint, forced. "Thank you," she said, then looked away.

The carriage drove on, gaining speed. He looked out the window. They passed Piccadilly toward Covent Garden and Piazza where women often roamed the streets and hooked their prey. But he was no better to judge anyone. More often than not, these young women had nowhere else to turn, the victims of cruel reality.

He looked back at the young woman again, the dichotomy of their realities slapping him in the face. Would she succumb to such depravity? He didn't like the answer his mind whispered to him.

There was a long stretch of silence as they passed Newgate Prison. He noticed the shift in the neighborhood, dilapidated and in much need of repairs. Within several turns, soot and dirt was visible on the buildings, along with debris scattered about on the streets. He turned his attention to the young woman sitting across from him. She was looking out the window too, obviously anxious to get home and attend to her mother.

But he said nothing and allowed her the silence that seemed necessary.

Blackthorn turned his attention to the familiar old bakery. A whore stood against the wall. Her clothes had been made of fine muslin, he observed. The hem was dirt ridden and there were stains on the skirt. Several strands were loose about the neck and ample bosom. When she caught sight of his carriage, she pulled away from the wall and donned a smile.

Beatrice looked at the familiar tattered building. "We're here, sir." She quickly opened the door, stepped out, and briskly walked straight to the door.

The sunlight illuminated a cruel reality before him. Several children in rags ran past the whore, shouting to one another as they chased a tiny puppy across the street. On the steps of the bakery sat an old woman holding something on her lap. Her hair was pulled back in a thick knot. Her gaze was cast downward as she rested her head on the old stone wall, as if too tired to move. But what he saw as he neared gripped him with melancholy that he wasn't accustomed to.

In her lap was a sleeping infant wrapped in a dirty blanket. He halted, his foot bolted to the floor as if it willed him to stop and take notice. He looked down at the baby, who very much needed bathing, and back at the old woman, who seemed to have exhausted herself too much to even care what was transpiring before her. The sight before him shattered the wall he'd built up and knocked him to his knees. Then it hit him. He'd been too busy immersed in his own thoughts to even notice the old woman was dead.

Holding a baby.

He'd seen much of the world, its darkness and cruelty; still one could never get used to this. The baby shifted and started to wail. First softly, but when no comfort came, its wail became louder and desperate. Blackthorn lowered himself and gingerly removed the woman's arm. Her body was beginning to stiffen, but being careful nonetheless, he gently picked up the baby in his arms. Lord, this wasn't a place for any child. Looking at the old woman one last time, he entered the house the girl had walked into with the infant in his arm.

Everyone turned to look at him.

Beatrice looked at him curiously, then faced her mother who was lying on the makeshift bed. All the children surrounded her as if waiting for her to open her eyes.

The youngest of the six, Francis, came running to him. "Are you here to help my mum?"

He knelt on one knee and tried his best to smile. "Yes."

The girl touched the baby's cheeks and smiled. "Her mother died a week ago. My mum told me her grandmamma is going to take care of her now."

No, my little one. Her grandmother is dead. "Did she?"

He didn't have the heart to say anything to the little girl. He walked over and handed the baby to Beatrice. She took the baby without hesitation. Blackthorn leaned in to their mother and touched her forehead, then felt the pulse on her neck. It was very faint, and she was still hot to the touch.

Just then the doctor walked into the house, then looked around as if he could not believe what he saw. But without further ado, he touched the woman's forehead. "How long has she had the fever?"

Beatrice answered, "For two days, sir."

The doctor shook his head.

"Will she be all right?" Blackthorn asked.

"At this point, all we can do is wait," he whispered to Blackthorn.

There was a long silence. All the children stood there looking around the room, fear brewing in their eyes. Francis was right by his side, as if he'd suddenly become her guardian, and a source of reassurance that he wasn't prepared to give to anyone.

But how could he not when there was so little hope for these children? "There is an older woman outside, sitting near the bakery. I will need you to take care of her," Blackthorn said to the doctor, who quickly got the meaning and nodded in reply. "Do what is necessary to give her the respectful burial she deserves." He turned to Beatrice. "The doctor will stay until your mother is better, I assure you that. Will you be all right in charge of the baby?"

She looked at him with fear in her eyes, but she nodded nonetheless.

"I won't be gone long."

When she heard these words, she smiled.

Blackthorn took no time in arranging for the orphaned baby and the children. In the two hours he was gone, he was able to secure a wet nurse for the baby, enough food for several days, and some new beddings for the mother. In addition, he would send word to his housekeeper to send one of the maids to assist the girls until their mother recovered from the fever.

When he finally returned, the doctor had no good news for him. Blackthorn asked the doctor to stay the night with the girls and told him to call on him as soon as there was news. With that, he departed to Mayfair, but as the carriage rolled away, he felt a sense of guilt.

What was this bloody guilt that seemed to eat away at him these days?

He knew the answer to that, didn't he?

Yes, he did.

Chapter 22

FROM HER WINDOW, Amelia looked at the sun waking on the horizon. The quill rolled off her fingers and onto the parchment, leaving a splatter of ink like ant trails on the ledger she was working on. Outside the window, hues of orange, gray, and blue splashed across the vastness of a dramatic canvas.

She hadn't slept much last night. Like a young, brokenhearted girl, she had tossed and turned, trying to understand Richard's meaning. Why hadn't he come to her room? Did he regret what had happened the night before?

Did it really matter?

The answer to her question was very clear. It didn't matter, because he had no intention of staying in London and she didn't want him to. She wanted independence, but spending all this time with Richard was confusing her.

Emotions only complicate things, she recalled her grandmother saying.

Still, there was something about him that shamefully

tugged at her heart. She could not stop that, and therefore, she must be very careful and keep her distance from the earl as much as she could.

Knock, knock, knock.

She opened her eyes; with her hand on her chest, she felt her heart beating wildly. She took a deep breath when she heard another knock, this time a bit louder. She smoothed her ivory-spotted muslin dress with both her hands and slowly rose to see who was at the door. But before she could reach for the knob, the door opened.

Mrs. Pots.

"I don't believe I gave you permission to enter."

"I didn't think you were in the room," Mrs. Pots blurted out. "I came to leave this on your desk." The woman looked around suspiciously as if someone were lurking about.

Amelia saw the letter in her hand and snatched it quite unladylike.

"It's from that earl of yours," she said.

"Oh?" Anticipation erupted.

"Will you be staying in during the evening?"

Amelia studied her chaperone for a minute. "Why?" she asked. "Will you be reporting that to my grandmother as well?"

Mrs. Pots' eyes narrowed. "I was merely asking, as now that you're engaged, the earl would no doubt want your company for a social gathering." She paused, and her gaze raked over Amelia. "If you ask my opinion, I doubt his—"

"I don't," Amelia blurted out. "And I'd watch your tongue if I were you. My grandmother may have hired you, but I am her granddaughter. Unless you care about your employment after she is gone, I suggest you tread very carefully with me." She hated treating anyone so poorly, but the woman brought out a side of her she didn't like. In the beginning, Amelia had tried kindness, thinking it might temper the woman's hatred and hostility toward her.

"Don't you threaten me. I have been in your grandmother's employment for nearly three decades." Mrs. Pots paused as if looking for the right words, the creases around her eyes softening as if she recalled a memory. "She trusts me implicitly."

"Is that why you are so cruel?"

"I don't know what you mean."

"You must feel threatened by me. Are you resentful somehow?"

"Don't be ridiculous," Mrs. Pots said, glaring at Amelia.

The woman turned on her heel and left the room before Amelia could form a rebuttal. She frowned, hope dissolving into nothingness.

Amelia quickly opened the letter and read it: *It's urgent that I speak with you. Meet me at Somersby Hall in an hour. If you are unable, send word with the time and date you can meet me. B*

The first thing that came to mind was Millie. Had he found her?

She grabbed a cloak, ordered her carriage to be ready, and instructed the butler that she may be gone a while and did not know when she would return.

It took over an hour to arrive at Somersby Hall. It had

started to rain as they drove along Oxford Street toward the outskirts of London. Much to her annoyance, the rain pelted down fiercely. She rested her head on the squab and closed her eyes, trying not to worry but it was no use.

When her carriage turned into the driveway of Somersby Hall, she saw a flicker of light emanating from the ground floor. Before the carriage came to a full halt, she saw Lord Blackthorn step out of the front door in a quick stride.

He quickly moved to speak with the driver and pulled the door open for her. Then, without a moment's rest, he linked his hand with hers and guided her into the house. Entering the foyer, she pulled her wet cloak off and handed it to the footman. "Has something happened? Why have you asked me to meet you here?"

Just then a loud, shrill cry echoed throughout the house.

Chapter 23

"**N**O, YOU CAN'T keep her." A voice shattered the momentary silence.

Amelia sped toward the voice. As she entered the parlor, she didn't expect to find what she saw before her. Six girls were scattered about the room and attempting to trap what looked to be an oversized rat that had been hit by lightning. One girl who looked to be maybe fifteen was holding an infant in her arms trying to keep away from the children. It seemed the tiny creature had been dipped in mud as the room was spattered all over, from the rug to the furniture. A little girl who looked to be no more than five ran to the frightened dog.

"I won't give 'er up. I won't," the little girl shouted, attempting to protect the creature from the other girls that surrounded it like vultures.

Amelia scanned the mud-splattered room. One of the girls tried to snatch the dog from the little girl's arms. When she succeeded, the little girl teared up and started to sob. "I found her. Give her back to me."

Instantly, Amelia went to the older girl and looked at her with a smile. "It's all right." Amelia took the dog from her grip and walked over to the one crying. Wiping the tears off her cheek, Amelia said, "There is no need to cry, darling. I won't let them take her away from you."

"Do you promise?" She cuddled the puppy as if afraid to let it go.

"I promise." Amelia gave her a wide smile. "They will have to answer to me first."

The little girl smiled, but her lips quivered.

"What is wrong, darling?" Amelia asked, caressing her head.

"Where is Mummy? When is she coming back? I want to show her my new puppy." The little girl looked at her, tears falling from her eyes. Amelia looked up at Blackthorn, and the look he gave her made her stomach drop. Her heart ached for the girl.

Amelia smiled at the little girl. "You stay here and take care of your new puppy. I will return shortly. I promise." With that, she left the parlor and walked toward the back of the house as quickly as she could without running.

Hot tears burned her eyes. She didn't know what had hit her. One minute she had been consoling the girl and the next this utter sadness had come over her without warning. She could not stop it, not even if her life depended on it. This sadness felt like a massive wave that crashed into her, and she had no desire to hold it back.

She heard heavy footfalls behind her, but she didn't look back.

"Amelia," she heard, but she didn't stop.

When Richard reached out for her, she said, "No." Amelia signaled with her hand for him to stop where he was. "Please . . . I just . . . I just . . . need a moment." She turned to look away, a lump of emotion ready to burst. Tears fell before she could stop them.

Blackthorn pulled her into his arms and held her and she melted in his embrace. She felt his hard chest somehow protecting her. She let the tears fall, soaking his coat. Her head rested gently on the column of his neck, which had a warm musky scent mixed with woody earth. Then, without thinking, she looked up at him. Before she knew what she was doing, her lips found his. The warmth of his now-familiar lips ignited desires in her again, but she willed herself to stop.

He wiped away the last remaining tears. "Are you all right?"

"I will be," she said. "Whose children are they?"

"My brother knew their father. They were friends, but he died in the war, so my brother made sure each month they received provisions and some money to take care of the girls. I didn't know about them until recently."

"That was very brave and thoughtful of your brother," she said. "But that doesn't explain why they are here."

"Their mother passed away today. They have nowhere else to go," he said. "My mother is at Blackthorn Hall, so I couldn't take them there, and my London house was not equipped for all these children."

She smiled. "I see." Richard truly had a good heart. Bloody hell, it was going to be hard to forget this man.

"I need a few days to arrange to have the girls' welfare in order."

Amelia didn't protest. It would be good to have some laughter in her life. In truth, while she may have benefitted from her grandmother's generosity, she had more in common with these girls and knew firsthand what it felt like to be abandoned and hungry.

"Where will they go?" she asked.

"I am hoping there are families in the village that might consider taking the girls and the baby."

"You intend to separate them?" The idea that these girls might have to grow up without each other, after losing their mother, hit her hard.

He sighed. "As much as I'd like the girls to remain together, it is likely they won't. It's a lot of mouths to feed for a single family."

He was right, of course. She looked in the direction of the girls' muffled voices coming from the hallway. The thought of them separated for the rest of their lives gripped her with uneasiness. Guilt, regret, and anger burned in the pit of her stomach. She knew the feeling all too well, didn't she? No doubt they would be forced to work menial labor, or worse, subjected to male brutality and forced to sell their bodies for food, uneducated with no prospects of a hopeful future. She could not in good conscience be a witness to it all. She could never forgive herself.

"I will take them."

Richard's brows rose in surprise, his mouth pulling into a thin line. "What?"

"They can stay with me."

"You are serious."

"Indeed." She looked away for a moment. "There is enough room here and I will have the means to support these girls once I inherit."

"I admire your courage, truly, but I think you should consider the ramifications of what you are taking on."

Ramifications? She was very aware of what she was taking on. "I am grateful for your concern, really I am. But I have made my decision and nothing you say will deter me from doing what is right for these girls." She turned to walk away, but he gripped her arm and pulled her to him. She turned to look at him. Those fascinating and most annoying eyes observed her.

"Why are you doing this?" he asked.

She looked at him thoughtfully. "If I don't, who will? You?"

A look of concern and confusion splashed across his chiseled face. Of course he didn't understand. How could he? It wasn't his fault that he was born into privilege. His actions thus far had revealed him to be an honorable and charitable man, but a *man* nonetheless. He could never understand her plight, nor her desire to make her own choices and live by her own rules. Their eyes met again. Why the bloody hell was he looking at her as though she were a lost puppy?

"You cannot carry the weight of the world on your shoulders, no matter how much you want the best for these girls. Give me a few days to find a family who is willing to take them."

She sighed. What were the chances that one family would take all of them? "Only if they can stay together."

He sighed. "I will try."

"They stay together," she said again. "Or they will remain here with me."

"I could forbid it."

She watched him. He may be serious, but so was she. "You could," she said. "But I don't think you will, or you would never have brought them here."

As soon as Mrs. Pots entered Sir Kendall's study, he walked over to her and undid her hair. Watching it fall, he put the pin on his desk.

"What have you discovered?" he said. He wasn't particularly fond of women his age, but this was a means to an end.

"She's gone to Somersby Hall with that earl," she said, sitting down opposite him at his desk. "Oh, I like that," she said when he kissed her neck.

Kendall reached under her shirt and touched Mrs. Pots. She moaned the way she had when he touched her there before. The woman was under his spell, and he meant to use that to his advantage.

"Did you hear anything?"

"No," she said. "But I can always write to her grandmother about her behavior." She smiled at him. "In fact, the good news is, I already have."

What good are you if you can't give me information I can use? "Good girl," he said as he slowly bent her over his desk, lifted her skirt, and lowered his breeches.

Chapter 24

THE CHAOS OF getting everyone fed and ready for bed took nearly three hours. Miss Knight helped bathe the children. Blackthorn made sure the housekeeper prepared the rooms and lit the fireplaces for the night.

He paused at the base of the stairs. A momentary stillness engulfed him as buried memories flooded through him. Somehow being here with these children filled him with guilt and grief. Perhaps it was because his brother had wanted to fill this house with his children. It should be Max standing here with his own children. Not only had he been a dutiful son, he had stood for all that was good in this world. He would have been a good father.

When Max had suddenly died from an unrelenting fever, Blackthorn had blamed himself. Max may have been older, but he'd always been weak and fragile. There was nothing Blackthorn could do but torture himself with the knowledge that he hadn't done enough. Suddenly, this house had become a cold and lifeless place.

His thoughts turned to the children now sound asleep in their warm beds. The truth was, Francis's laughter seemed to magically lift the heavy burden that lingered in his heart. Early that night, the young cherub had said that it was silly to call the infant "Baby" and had wanted to name her Bell instead. When he'd asked her why, she'd replied, "All my sisters have little sisters, except me. I want *her* to be *my* little sister." She went on to explain that since their surname was Bell, she felt it was fitting to give it to the baby so that she would be part of their family.

"So her name will be Bell Bell?" he'd asked.

She had giggled. "No, silly. Just Bell. *Our* Bell."

"I see," he'd said, touched. "Then Bell it is." He didn't have the heart to tell her Bell may not be with them for long. He would have to inquire about the baby's family soon. It would be difficult for the girls to lose her, but if the baby had a relative willing to take her in, he could not in good conscience deprive the infant of growing up with her own family.

Blackthorn slowly walked up the stairs and through the hallway. There he saw Miss Knight quietly step out of the children's room and close the door behind her. She was holding a taper candle, and the soft glow spilled to her neckline and down to her full bosom. Her lips pulled into a grin.

That smile. He could lose himself in her smile. For a moment, everything that anchored them to their duties seemed to fade away and fatigue set in.

"Are they asleep?" he whispered to her.

"Finally, yes," she replied, walking up to him.

"Good," he said. "You must be exhausted."

"I am, but right now they are safe. I worry about them losing their mother so suddenly."

Blackthorn watched her with confusion. He'd never met a woman more self-sacrificing than her. "For now, they have you . . .us. You can't take care of those around you if you aren't well."

"I agree," she said. "I want so much for the children to have a home, and someone to care for them." She paused, as if she wasn't sure she should continue. "But I fear the ramifications of their mother's death haven't fully reached them. The eldest girl, I believe her name is Beatrice, well she is awfully quiet. Too quiet, I'm afraid."

"They have you for now," he said again. "I'm here to do whatever I can."

Her gaze softened with a smile. "I thank you for that, but I fear it's not enough."

Cook had told him how Amelia's her mother had sent her away and left London.

"Do you have a moment?" she asked.

"Of course."

"We can talk in the parlor," she said, leading the way.

Once they were ensconced in the parlor, he quietly shut the door and lit three taper candles on the candelabra, setting it on the side table next to the chairs. He watched her as the soft glow of candlelight splashed across her face. Several locks of hair fell loose, and dark brown stains on the sleeve of her cream dress reminded him of the night they'd had. With all the fineries and servants at her disposal, she

215

had chosen to be there for these children. Generous to a fault, and she asked for nothing in return, he thought with a tug in his heart.

She blinked again, looking at him with those chestnut-brown eyes. She looked so fragile in the gleam of the candlelight. How many times had he fantasized about having her in his bed, kissing her, all of her? He wanted her. He wanted to feel her hands on him, all of him. In the intimacy of the room, he momentarily forgot why he'd asked her here. Oh God, how he wanted to kiss away her troubles and protect her from the demons she was fighting.

She walked over to the couch and sat down, her hands folded on her lap. "About the other night . . ."

"Yes," he said with a smile, knowing exactly what she was referring to. "Go on."

"I don't think it should happen again."

"You think it was a mistake?"

"No," she said. "I mean, yes."

"Which is it?"

"It was . . . a mistake. I think it is best if we don't get physical for the sake of the arrangement."

"It's too late for that, don't you think?" His eyes fell to her chest, taking in her perfectly formed bosom rising and falling in anticipation of what was coming. She was watching him carefully, forming her retort.

"I don't believe so," she said bravely. "Just because we shared one night of union, that does not mean we can't remain friends."

"For the sake of our arrangement?"

"Yes," she said with a defiant glare. Her lips thinned. "I am quite tired and would like to retire if you don't mind."

"One more thing. That man in the alley, you said you didn't know him."

"I don't," she said. "Why?"

Her gaze was observant, as if to scrutinize his intentions while waiting to see what he might say next. It was difficult to forgo his spy training. Since he'd left university, it had been ingrained in him to watch, observe, and extract as much information as possible in a given time. Hiding behind the façade he'd erected with such precision, he sometimes forgot who the hell he was. This habit was hard to break.

"I believe the man in the alley may have been Sir Kendall."

"Really?" she said. "Why do you think he may be the one?"

"Millie is carrying Philip's child, according to Cook. It would make sense that he doesn't want you to find her." Blackthorn feared Kendall may have already disposed of Millie since she was carrying Philip's child. This knowledge would surely humiliate Kendall since his aim was to be part of Society and be accepted as one of them.

"Do you think he might hurt her?" she asked when he didn't reply.

"I don't know." He knew very well a man like Kendall would not think twice about hurting a whore, but he was not about to worry Amelia more than he already had.

She touched her necklace, and tears filled her eyes. Wiping them away, she said, "I am sorry. I've never cried so much in my life. I learned quickly to dry my tears when I was in Scotland."

"Your grandmother didn't allow tears?"

"No," she said. "She used to say, 'Emotions only complicate things.'"

There was much truth to that, he concluded. Yet he could not stop himself from touching her. He reached out and pulled her into his arms.

She searched his eyes for comfort. His eyes softened and he kissed her gently on her lips. This extraordinary man made her wish for things she had never thought possible for her. Richard shifted and kissed the curve of her neck. Without forethought, she positioned herself and pulled at his shirt. Her hand worked to untie his cravat, and she pulled it until it came free. She didn't want to be the timid, innocent girl who waited for a man to take charge of making love to her.

She saw the hunger in his eyes, burning, wanting, and waiting impatiently to see what she'd do next. The other night, she had told him to undress in front of her and he had. Oh, how glorious that had felt. A sense of control over this man aroused her, thrilled her. She didn't allow herself to think, this one last time.

Quickly, he pulled off her drawers and tossed it, then slowly proceeded to unclasp the garters and slid the silk stockings off one by one. He pulled the dress off her and began to untie the cross-lace on her corset until she was free from it. Donned in a see-through chemisette, her perky nipples rubbed on the fabric. She saw the heat in his eyes and she smiled in approval and slowly pulled her chemisette off.

He looked at her with an intensity she'd seen when he'd

been with her alone in her bedchamber. When he kissed her, it was hot and wanting and the sudden feel of his silky tongue licking the tips of her nipples one at a time made her body melt, and she moaned. Sucking, licking, he continued until she was whispering his name again and again.

Richard gathered her on his lap and his hands slowly glided up her thighs toward her buttocks. She inched closer and positioned herself above the tight mound beneath her, and all the while he was kissing her neck, chest, and lower… Then lower still until he was right above her nipples.

She liked this. No, she loved this feeling. This sensation was intoxicating, and her body seemed to know what to do without her command. His hand shifted downward between her legs and touched the soft spot there. He was deliciously stroking her sex, and she moaned softly. Oh, what was he doing to her? His hands did magical things to her and she couldn't think. She couldn't help but drink in the sensations he was creating with his wonderful hand. Again, he sucked on the rosy peak of her breast with demanding mastery, while her hands ran through the thick of his hair.

Is this how he made love to all his lovers? No wonder women loved him. Her arms wrapped around his neck to pull him closer to her, and he kissed her gently at first until his mouth covered hers hungrily, demanding her to open her lips. His tongue slid in and explored her mouth like he had been deprived, while his hands stroked the nub between her legs.

He broke the kiss. "Let's take it slow, my sweet."

She shook her head. "I don't want it slow."

His gaze met hers with the intensity and focus of a hunter in action. He shifted and gently placed her on the couch and lowered himself.

"What are you doing?" she said.

He gave her a naughty smile. "I am going to please you again. You liked it enough the other night."

So he did remember, she thought with a smile.

He lifted the skirt up higher to her hips, and slowly kissed her inner thigh, leaving her sex throbbing in need as he moved upward to kiss her there. She arched her back as his stroke became hot and her need for more became unbearable. No words could explain the sensation that ignited there. Even if she wanted to stop, she couldn't. His tongue dabbed, stroked, and licked that sensitive part of her body until she thought she would burst with pleasure. But something was holding her back. This intense feeling felt frighteningly uncontrollable.

"Let go," he said, looking up at her. "Release for me, darling."

Instinctively, her fingers forked through his hair as his hands cupped her buttocks to get a better angle. In an instant, the last stroke of his soft mouth did it, and she heard herself cry out loud in an intensifying release that left her feeling blissfully happy.

Was this what all women experienced? Was this what she'd been missing? The one time she'd been with a man hadn't brought her anything close to this kind of pleasure, lust, or whatever you wanted to call it. While her chest heaved, he came up to lie with her on the couch and gave her a passionate kiss. Their bodies intertwined like a vine, and they were one.

She ran her hand over his firm chest and reached down to his swollen manhood, and he smiled. Undoing the buttons, she reached in and touched him. He shifted so that she could have a better angle as she explored the firmness of him as if she were exploring a new land where she'd never been. Full and ready. She stroked it again and again, and in the depth of his low groan, he searched for her mouth and claimed it with hunger. She gave herself freely to his need. Her need. She liked this control over him. Loved it. She touched the tip of his erection and stroked it gently with her thumb, again and again, watching his hard expression all the while, never looking away. Within several seconds, he released with a low moan that made her smile.

For several minutes, they both remained still. He reached down and grabbed her hand, kissing the palm before holding her hand on his chest.

She helped him wipe himself off, and he pulled her close to kiss her again. "I can get used to this," he said, helping her sit up next to him. He released the ornate pin in her hair and her hair came tumbling down.

"What's wrong?" she asked, looking at his expression. "You're not happy?"

"You're beautiful," he said. Pulling her close to him, he wrapped her in his arms and stroked her bare back, moving lower and lower, until he stiffened. It was then she realized why he didn't move. *Oh, no, this was not what she wanted.*

"Let me see your back," he said, his tone grave and low.

She tried pulling her bodice up, but he wouldn't let her. She slowly lowered her bodice and turned her back to him reluctantly.

For several seconds he was silent.

Too silent.

"Who has done this to you?" His tone was a mixture of disgust and loathing.

"Do you have to ask?" she replied, turning to face him. His expression changed and there was sadness in his eyes. "My grandmother," she said. When he didn't reply, she continued. "My grandmother does not tolerate misbehavior."

"You are not property to be enslaved or beaten," he said angrily.

"She thinks otherwise." The words came out in a whisper.

"Has she done anything else?"

More than Amelia could count, but she was not about to relive the horrible events. "No."

He pulled her closer to him and kissed all six thick scars that ran nearly two feet in length across her back. When her grandmother had discovered that for months Amelia had spent her free time with the young man who worked the stables and took care of the horses, her grandmother had raged. Amelia had not been allowed to eat for two days.

On the third day, she had been allowed water and porridge and continued with her regular schedule, but that hadn't stopped the tears because she had discovered that her grandmother had relieved the young man without compensation. She had been forbidden to speak with the servants from then on. Her life got lonelier as each day passed.

Her grandmother had blamed her for everything. She had thought about running away, but where would she go? To her mother, who didn't want her? She hadn't even known if her mother was alive. To her relatives she didn't have? Where? The glimmer of hope that she may buy her freedom one day, and see Millie again, had kept her there.

With everything Richard had done for her, the least she could do was explain. "I stayed because I knew if I did as she asked, I would have my freedom one day. She can't live forever."

"Is this the reason you have chosen to live out your life alone?"

"I won't be alone. I have friends," she said. More like one friend, but he didn't need to know that. "Kate has been a true friend to me."

He nodded as if to sympathize. "Trust is earned. I don't give it away easily, and I sense from your tone that you are the same." He paused. "This brutality should never have happened to you."

His jaw twitched, and he gazed at her most seriously.

"What's wrong?" she said.

"This will never happen to you again. Your grandmother will never hurt you again."

She smiled at him and gave him a kiss. What kind of life had he had? What had his childhood been like? She assumed all aristocrats did as they pleased, when they pleased, and in the manner they deemed fit. But he was different. For the first time, she truly saw the depth of his compassion, his generosity and kindness. There was something about him that was sad, too. She'd seen it but hadn't cared to see what was in front of her, for survival.

She watched him, really looked at him, and noticed something she hadn't seen before. She had noticed the scar on his temple earlier, but now there was a visible mark below his ear, about an inch long. Her eyes traveled down and saw a scar below his shoulder blade.

"Where did you get this?" she asked, reaching out to touch it.

"I was attacked with a knife."

"By whom?"

"Street gang."

For someone who reprimanded her for lurking in dangerous places, he must have spent quite a lot of time there to get hurt the way he had, which made her wonder why he had been there in the first place. "And this?" she said, pointing to the round scar.

"Bullet wound, in the army. I was young."

She kissed it. "Where did you go after you left the army?"

"I went to work for the Home Office."

Her opinion of him had been quite premature. She'd thought he'd lived a life of luxury and privilege in the safe confines of his home, but she was wrong. "Doing what?"

He was quiet for a moment. "I will tell you more about it tomorrow."

"You know everything about me," she said. "Please, I desire to know."

He sighed heavily. "I went on diplomatic missions for the Regent in the interest of my country."

Hum . . . interesting. "What does that mean, exactly?"

"My sweet, please . . . I'm tired and I'd like to sleep with you next to me."

She thought about what he had revealed to her. It sounded awfully like— "Were you a spy?"

He said nothing for a moment. "I like to keep that part of my life behind me."

She had been so completely wrong about this man. He was honorable, kind, and generous. And now she was falling for him.

Which was not an option for her. If only her heart could agree with that.

Chapter 25

THE RIDE BACK to her townhouse was a silent one, and she was thankful for it. She needed to think; she needed space. He held her hand in his and gently stroked it.

Richard ordered the driver to park the carriage around the back by the mews so that she could sneak in through the servants' quarters. This was becoming a habit she needed to quickly remedy before she got caught.

"Let's get you inside, shall we?"

She allowed him to help her off the carriage, and together they walked up to the back door. It was hours past midnight.

When they reached the door, he pulled out something from an inside coat pocket and wedged it into the lock. With a quick twist, as if he'd done this a hundred times, the door unlocked. Curious, she watched him. Where had he learned to do that?

He pulled out something else from his inside coat pocket. "Keep this under your pillow, loaded." It was the pistol he used the night they met. "Go in and lock the door behind you."

She knew he stood there until she was safety ensconced in her house before she heard the clip-clopping of the carriage driving away. Removing her shoes, she walked past the narrow hallway and passed the kitchen. Hearing the whispers of servants near the servants' dining room, she slipped into the kitchen and listened.

"Has Miss Knight returned?"

"No," the maid said. "If ye ask me, no respectable man in his right mind would marry 'er." Pause. "There is somethin' strange going on 'bout here if ye ask me."

"Well, I like the lady," the housekeeper said.

"Of course ye'd say that," the maid said. "Ye like everybody."

"Never ye mind. Go to sleep."

No respectable man would marry her. There was so much truth in that remark. Would Richard have made love to her if he knew she was the daughter of a whore? Would he have agreed to this arrangement? He might have, since the inheritance was a significant sum, but would he respect her? Say the things he had said to her?

She heard the footsteps slowly fade away. She tiptoed upstairs as fast as she could before she was noticed. Instead of going straight to her room, she quietly tiptoed to Kate's room next to hers. She pressed her ear to the door and listened. It was late, but Kate usually stayed up late. She heard nothing, but faint candlelight spilled under her door. Knocking softly, she pushed the door open slightly. There, she saw Kate sound asleep on her bed holding a parchment in her hand.

Amelia tilted her head to get a better look and saw that it was a letter. She looked closer and saw the name Jonathan. She couldn't see the rest of his name because Kate's thumb was in the way. She inched closer but halted when Kate shifted in her bed.

Quietly leaning over, she blew out the candles, one by one. Before the last one went out, Kate shifted, slowly opening her eyes.

"You're back," she said, rubbing her eyes. "What time is it?"

"After midnight." Amelia sat on the edge of the bed. "Go back to sleep. We can talk tomorrow."

Kate observed her. "What's wrong?"

"Nothing is wrong." Amelia paused. Everything was wrong.

"You're lying," she said. "Don't you know I can always tell when you are lying to me?"

Kate was right. Before her departure, Amelia had left a note with Kate saying she had some matters to remedy, so she filled in the details about what had transpired tonight, except the kiss. "Lord Blackthorn wants to find a home for the six orphans and a newborn baby."

Kate raised her brow, sitting up on her bed. "What will you do?"

"What else can I do?"

"Oh, Amelia, you can't possibly be thinking of keeping them."

"Lord Blackthorn is looking for relatives or families that are willing to take them in."

"And if he can't?"

Amelia knew what she would do. It wasn't even a question in her mind. She couldn't think of the poor children in the streets, begging for money or stealing like Millie had and resorting to selling themselves just to feed their hungry bellies. What kind of life would that be?

"That is a lot of responsibility for one person."

"I cannot abandon these children. They will no doubt end up in the streets."

"Well, let's just hope his lordship finds someone before you end up being a mother of seven girls." Kate pulled the covers off and sat down next to her friend. "You know I will be here to help you in any way I can, but you really need to think this through before you make a decision."

While Kate didn't share much of her past with her, Amelia respected that. She had a past also, one that she wasn't ready to reveal to anyone, not unless she was willing to pay the ultimate price.

Amelia's eyes drifted to the letter Kate was holding. "Who is it from?"

Kate quickly folded the letter. "Oh, this," she said and walked over to the small writing table. "It's nothing."

All Amelia knew of Kate's life before she arrived in Scotland three years ago after her husband passed away was that she had inherited a castle from a distant cousin, so she'd moved to Scotland to start over. Kate's idea of a perfect life was fine dining and hotels.

"Never mind me. You've been spending a lot of time with the earl." Kate smiled widely.

She nodded. "I have. He is . . . a very nice man."

"Nice?" Kate said, giving her a sideways glance. "Did something happen between you two?"

"Of course not."

"You're having feelings for the earl, aren't you?"

She bit her lip. "Don't be absurd. I barely know the man."

"Oh, honey," Kate said, touching Amelia's folded hands. "Enjoy it a little. You can't live your life as a nun."

The thought was infectious. "Emotions will only complicate things between us in the end, and, in my case, it serves no purpose."

"Does he have feelings for you?"

"Men like him won't allow their hearts to dictate their lives. Eventually, all that will matter is an heir and money for his coffer." Even she knew that was a lie.

"If that's the case, it should make things quite easy." Kate watched her. "But that's not what you want, is it?"

"I want my independence," she said. "That hasn't changed."

"But do you want him?"

"I don't know," she said. "He is very clear about leaving London. He does not want to be committed to anyone."

"Does he still feel that way?"

"Does it really matter?"

She would not be ready to contemplate that idea any time soon.

Blackthorn didn't leave. He ordered his driver to go home. Donning his thick outer coat, he walked the perimeter of the street to make sure he didn't see anyone lurking about her townhouse. Then, from across the street, he watched Amelia's window. The flickering light in the room stayed lit for no more than thirty minutes before she snuffed it. He was compelled to sneak into her room and slip under the covers with her, but he needed to think and clear his head.

He knew very well he would leave this woman when the time came. There was no doubt about that. The goal had always been the same, and he didn't like the power she had over him.

This lust and hunger for this woman was nothing he had ever felt for anyone.

Yet, he knew he would leave her. He never had trouble leaving. Actually, he was very good at it.

He needed a damn drink.

Yes, that sounded awfully good right now.

Chapter 26

BLACKTHORN WAS DRUNK. Damn bloody drunk. And he didn't wish to go home. The one drink at the tavern turn into two, then five until he lost count.

Now, he wanted Amelia. He wanted to see her.

Here and there, images of her materialized, causing him to stop what he was doing. Or he imagined talking with her about his day. No doubt she'd argue with him. Now and again, the idea of having a real family pulled at his heart. But then there was something else, something that troubled him deeply today. Normally on this day, he drowned in his grief alone.

Strange that he'd think of Amelia on this day of grief. After all, today was Max's birthday. He would have been three and thirty today.

Before Max's death, Blackthorn had planned to live the rest of his life abroad. But with Max gone, his plan to remain abroad had been indefinitely cancelled, and he'd found himself in London running a household with a title that wasn't supposed to be his.

All this should have been Max's. Rightly so; his brother had deserved peace and some happiness. But instead, his brother was dead and Blackthorn was here. Never once had he had the desire to remain in London, for anyone or anything.

But now, all that had changed.

He had never known how it felt to have a real family. His father had been too busy with his elder brother. His mother hadn't liked the distractions of London and preferred the quiet in Bath. At most, he had only seen his family once a year. The rest of the year he spent traveling or at Eton. Now, Amelia was stirring feelings in him he hadn't known he was capable of.

He wasn't sure why he had returned to stand in front of her stylish Mayfair townhouse, rain pelting down on his cool face, like a common thief watching his victim. He could easily slip into the house. God knew he'd done that enough times to do it blindfolded.

He'd count to ten and if the candlelight still burned, he'd slip inside.

One. Two. Three. Four.

His heart pounded against his chest, breathing life into his body.

Five. Six. Seven.

Just then, she walked up to the window and pulled the curtains aside. Looking up at Amelia, he quietly counted.

Eight. Nine.

Her gaze lowered and she saw him.

She didn't move.

Neither did he.

Then she slipped away. A minute later, she opened the front door and pulled him inside in an instant.

Holding his hand, she led him up the stairs, looking to see if Mrs. Pots was lurking about. Once up the stairs, she rushed him into her room and clicked the door locked.

Only then did she face him. "You are soaking wet," she whispered. "Come by the fire and take those clothes off before you catch your death."

His gaze lifted, but he said nothing. One by one, he pulled off each layer—first his cravat, then his coat and his shirt that clung to his skin, his muscles flexing as he worked. Then he pulled off his boots, his breeches, and before she knew what was happening, he was standing there in his underthings that barely covered his manhood.

From the fine cords of his neck down to his well-built chest that glistened from the rain in the glow of the warm fire, and to his hard stomach, he was a delicious specimen of a man. She eyed the scars on his shoulder and chest, thinking with tenderness of all he'd been through safeguarding his country.

She forced herself to focus. Walking to her bed, she pulled off the sheet and handed it to him. She walked over and grabbed a chair sitting against the wall and placed the wet clothes there. She tried to think of anything, anyone other than the naked man standing before her.

"Are you trying to catch your death?" She realized he hadn't said a single word to her. Her heart lurched, afraid that he may have some news she didn't want to hear. Had something happened to the girls? Millie? Or the baby? Why else would he be here at this hour in the rain? "Is everything all right?"

He stood near the hearth just looking at her, the look on his face a mixture of torment and desperation. Something akin to a broken soul, and she desperately wanted to kiss away the pain. Something had happened, she saw it in his eyes.

"Sit," she said, prompting him to sit by the warm fire. She joined him. "Are you warm enough?" When he nodded, she sighed in relief and smiled.

He was indeed a beautiful man and nothing about him was ordinary. His eyes looked deeply into her and she melted into them. *Oh, God, why must you look at me like that?* The pull in her heart was so fierce she feared he might see right through her, so she did the only thing she could think of—talk. After all, this was a dangerous game he was playing, and while she knew he needed to leave, she realized she would be gravely disappointed if he did.

"What happened? Are the girls all right?"

"Must we speak of the girls tonight?"

"You've been drinking." She saw the glaze over his eyes, that drunken stupor, but it wasn't cheap gin; rather there was a hint of a floral scent.

"I had a glass or two." He was looking at the fire now.

"Something is troubling you," she said. "What has happened?" Perhaps he didn't want to be alone. She could hardly believe that a man like him had trouble finding company.

"My brother would have been three and thirty today."

235

Her face drained of blood. Oh, no. How terrible to have to be alone on his late brother's birthday. She kissed his temple and stroked his back. "I'm sorry about your brother. It must have been very painful."

She noticed his face, his twitching jaw. There was sadness in his eyes, but it was subtle. "You must miss him very much."

"My brother should be here." He looked down at his hands as if rubbing at an invisible stain he couldn't get rid of. "He was a good man, a good son to my parents." He sighed heavily.

She pressed her head to his chest and heard the thump, thump, thump. Slow and steady. Surely she knew how it felt to be unwanted by the very parents who gave you life. There was a connection there between them, one that she could not deny any longer.

They remained embraced, then slowly he dropped the thin sheet, pulling her nightgown over her head. "I like you like this," he said. He kissed her neck, breasts, and down further until he was kissing her abdomen. He stayed there for a moment, and her fingers forked in his hair. In their loneliness and grief, they united.

He stood up and kissed her. The softness of his lips lingered, and she didn't want him to stop.

"Stay," she heard herself say. "Stay with me tonight."

The intensity in his eyes shook her and the prolonged anticipation was unbearable. Her heart leaped and raced, in part from wanting to soothe his sorrow and slake her craving for him. He picked her up in his arms and carried her to the bed.

Oh, God . . . kiss me. Let me wipe away your sorrows, she thought. She'd been dreaming of those lips since she opened her eyes this morning. She had found herself giddy and humming a tune she wasn't even familiar with, feeling light and contented. Mrs. Pots had taken notice of her mood and asked her what was wrong with her.

Yes, yes, yes. Kiss me. The smell of rain and the faint aroma of earthy cologne playfully aroused her senses with an all-consuming urgency. This need for him was something completely foreign to her.

As he worked to release her of her underthings, he kissed her nipples. The throbbing ache between her legs was unbearable. Then he spread her legs and entered her. She gasped as he filled her. Full and soft, he moved in a rhythmic motion as her legs came around him. Slow at first, then faster and faster until he came inside her and they both collapsed onto the bed, gasping for air.

She was shocked by how her body had responded to him so quickly: the pain of that initial thrust and the pleasure of him inside her, and everything in between. Her breath came short as she ran her hands over his chest. My God, was it even possible to feel the way she was feeling now? As childish as it sounded, if she were dreaming, she'd didn't want to awake.

Lying next to her, he pulled up the sheet and wrapped his arms around her. He kissed her temple. "Sleep, my sweet."

She couldn't sleep now. There were so many emotions running through her that it was impossible for her to sleep. She sensed he wasn't sleepy either. After several minutes, she said, "We need to talk."

"Now?" he said. "I'm not in the right frame of mind to discuss anything, my sweet."

"If I don't do it now, I won't be able to later," she said. "I need to settle this…this thing between us."

"All right," he said, looking at her.

"What is this between us? I need to be sure so that I know what to expect."

"What do you think this is?"

"I don't know what this is…that is the problem."

"I see," he said, sitting up and sighing. He ran his hand though his hair. "You are the one who wants independence, to be free of men."

"I do and that hasn't changed."

"Then what is the problem?" he said.

"I don't know, this thing between us is making me confused."

"Would you rather I not touch you anymore?"

"Yes," she said. "I mean no. I don't know."

"I never lied to you," he said. "I will get an annulment and leave London. That plan hasn't changed."

She said nothing, and his mouth was tight and uninviting. She felt the distance between them stretch for hundreds of miles. "You don't need to say anything."

"I think I do," he said. "I have never considered marriage. Not before and not now. Believe me when I say a real marriage isn't something I can give you. It will not end well between us."

"I think you need to go," she whispered.

Chapter 27

IN THE EVENING, Philip Kendall rushed into his father's study with a look of intent. Sir Kendall looked at his son in amusement. There was a determined look about him. Good, perhaps he'd finally decided to grow up.

"Father, I have news," he said.

"Oh?" Sir Kendall said, closing his thick ledger book. "Tell me of this news, son."

Philip inhaled deeply. "I am to be a father."

Kendall heard the words, but it took a moment for them to sink in. What exactly did Philip mean he was going to be a father? Had he impregnated Lady Lucinda? If he had, most likely the family would have kept that information private until after the wedding day. "Go on . . ." Sir Kendall cautiously said.

Philip looked squarely at his father, straightened up, and said, "I cannot marry Lady Lucinda. It is only right that I marry the mother of my—"

Philip's head whipped around as his father's hand met

his cheek. Kendall was burning with rage and he was ready to strangle his idiot son. What in God's name was he thinking? The thought that his son was stupid enough to make such a statement struck him dumb momentarily. "Are you mad?"

Philip glared at him as if he were looking at a stranger. "I can't marry Lucinda when I know another is carrying my child."

Damn bloody fool. "I know about the damn baby. And, no, you *will not* marry the whore. What in God's name is this world coming to?"

Philip glared at his father in horror. "This baby is *mine*."

"No, it isn't," Kendall said. "You are to have nothing to do with them, do you understand me?"

Philip stood there, his eyes wide open as if he were seeing his father for the first time. "I will not—"

"Listen carefully, boy," Kendall barked. "If you make any attempt to marry the whore, I will strip you of every comfort, every penny, and every connection, do you understand me? You will have no funds and will be left to beg for your food in the streets."

"How can you say such things? This is your grandchild."

"Enough," he shouted. "As far as I am concerned, this whore could have spread her legs for dozens of men. There is no proof this *thing* is yours."

"She isn't a whore. There is much good in her that you don't see. How can I ignore what I must do?"

"I have heard enough," he bellowed, pounding his fist on his desk. "She is insignificant, nobody, and therefore, this child is of no concern to you. Duty to *your* family. Honoring *your* family name. That is all that matters. You will marry Lady Lucinda, or I will throw you out. You will starve, do you understand?"

Philip looked at his father in shock, utterly speechless. Then Philip squared his shoulders and said, "That is an impossibility, Father, since I have already informed the lady of my decision."

"Not if I have anything to do about it." This was that bitch's doing.

You are going to pay dearly, Amelia, if it's the last thing I do.

Once his son left, Kendall walked up to the attic where Millie was kept. He'd had plans to move her before the baby came, but it seemed he had no choice but to get rid of her now before his son did something he would regret and ruined their future.

Opening the attic door, he went in. But what Kendall didn't realize was that Philip was on his trail, in part from curiosity and suspicion after speaking with Lord Blackthorn.

Kendall entered the room and grabbed Millie by the hair and she screamed, begging him to let go of her. With a hard slap, he ordered her to keep her mouth shut. Then he proceeded to drag her down the hallway where his son had witnessed the scene hidden in one of the empty rooms.

"You and that damn baby are going to pay."

Chapter 28

AMELIA COULDN'T SLEEP. Not after what had
transpired tonight with Richard. So, she readied herself, pulled
on a pelisse and woke the driver to take her to Somersby Hall.

She couldn't possibly think at home, not when Richard
had been in her bed. Her head pounded and her heart ached.
*This is what you deserve after getting involved emotionally with
the earl.*

When she arrived at Somersby Hall, the old butler
greeted her in his nightclothes. She thanked him and went
up to the makeshift nursery. Being here brought purpose to
her, and a sense of peace.

She would make this her home.

Their home, she thought, as motherly instinct kicked in
and she looked at the precious baby sleeping soundly. The
wet nurse quietly peeked in.

"I'm just visiting," Amelia whispered to her. "How are
the children?"

"They are all finally asleep," the young nurse said.

"That's good."

Just then, she felt a tug on her pelisse. Looking down, she saw Francis Bell looking up at her.

Amelia lowered. "What is the matter, darling?"

Rubbing her eyes, Francis said, "I can't sleep."

"Come," the nurse said. "I will tuck you in."

"No," she said. "I want Mummy."

Something in Amelia ached when Francis said those words. How often had she wanted her mummy after she had been sent away?

"When is Mummy coming back?"

Amelia didn't have to heart to tell her the truth. "I am not sure, darling. Would you like me to tuck you in?"

Francis's lips quivered, and she teared up.

Amelia dried her tears. "It will be all right, Francis. Your sisters are here. I am here."

"Can I sleep with you?"

The nurse intervened, "Oh, honey... Miss Knight, I can—"

"It's all right," she said to the nurse, then looked at Francis. "Yes, you can sleep with me." Then Amelia picked her up in her arms and said goodnight to the nurse. The young girl wrapped her arms around Amelia's neck and Amelia nearly choked with emotion.

Once they were in the master bedchamber, Amelia tucked Francis under the blanket and lay next to her. "Go to sleep, darling."

Just then, the little curls bounced as Francis faced her. "Are you going to marry Mr. Richard?" That was the name she'd called him when he first brought the girls here.

Amelia nodded.

"Good," she said, smiling. "If Mummy doesn't come back, will you be my mummy? Mr. Richard can be my papa."

Tears formed. "We can talk tomorrow." She kissed the child's forehead, blew out the candle and wiped away the tears.

Several hours later, Amelia woke to shouting outside in the hallway. In a dreamy daze, she opened her eyes. It took a moment for her to realize where she was and who was next to her. Francis was still sound asleep. Then she noticed something strange. A burning smell of acid and wood mixed together.

Smoke, she said to herself in horror. "The children. The baby." She woke Francis and the little girl started to rub her eyes. "We have to go, Francis." Lifting the girl, Amelia carried her down the now-empty hallway.

The footman approached her and told her she must get out.

"What's happened?"

"Fire, miss. It's spreading fast," the footman said. "The townspeople are here trying to put out the fire, but it isn't helping."

"I need you to take Francis outside to safety." The girl resisted, but Amelia reassured her she would join her soon. Then she ran to the room where the girls were sleeping together. She woke them one by one.

"Beatrice," she said, walking over to the eldest of the sisters. "There is a fire," she told her as calmly as possible given the situation. "I need you to take the girls outside."

Beatrice quickly gathered the girls that were half asleep

and walked out of the room and down the narrow hallway. By now, the smoke was starting to fill the hallway. Choking, the girls scurried down the hall and walked down the stairs.

"The baby!" Amelia realized she'd forgotten the baby. Running to the nursery down the hall, smoke pinching her lungs, she covered her mouth, calling for the nurse. No answer.

Chaos ensued as she heard the men downstairs calling out to see if anyone was still in the house. She ran into the nursery and saw no baby. No nurse.

Running back into the hallway, she saw the three-legged dog barking at the end of the hallway. Running to the frightened dog, she scooped it up and ran toward the stairway. The smoke was becoming thick, and it stung her eyes. Fear engulfed her. Taking no time, she ran up the stairs to the third floor and into the hallway. She could hardly see. Coughing, she called out to the nurse. Grabbing her skirt, she placed in over her mouth to keep smoke from getting into her lungs.

Oh, please, please be all right.

Oh, my God. She saw hellish flames coming toward her like a wave on the ceiling. Fiery red. She stood there staring, momentarily unable to move. *Move, damn it,* her mind ordered. *Move.*

"Where are you?" she said, choking. Just then a figure approached from the thick smoke. It was a young footman. "We need to get you outside, miss."

"I need to find the nurse, the baby."

"I will search for them, miss. Go outside."

She ran down the hallway with the barking dog in her arms and by the time she reached the bottom of the stairs, she saw the red hellish flames approaching her. Finally outside, she saw a crowd of townspeople. Some watching. Others trying to help.

Several men were running inside and out with buckets of water, while women stood on the grass watching the fire eating away the house as the smoke thickened.

There was a loud crackling and a sizzling sound, followed by shattering glass. Amelia looked up to see the fire was spreading from the back of the house as the intense inferno arose from the roof and side windows. She could feel the heat from where she was.

Half of the upper floors were engulfed in fire now. The sky looked like hellfire, creating a bright light for miles. With each crack, each tumble as it ate away at the structure, her heart died inside.

She looked up to see the nurse holding the baby. "The baby is all right, miss."

Amelia took baby Bell into her arms and looked at the frightened girls, all watching her.

No time to cry.

"Is everyone out of the house?" she asked the housekeeper who was standing nearby with the scullery maid.

"I believe so," she answered, looking at the blazing fire.

As the fire consumed Somersby Hall, Amelia's heart was stripped of the dream that had kept her going for the last decade.

A home to call her own.

Sinful Pleasures

She watched the house slowly crumble into hot flames, and her heart broke into tiny pieces.

She felt defeated. Truly defeated.

Chapter 29

AMELIA WOKE SCREAMING.

Then, realizing the reality of her situation, she started to weep. Weep away the horrors of last night. Weep away her dream. Not bothering to sit up, she buried her face in her pillow.

Last night, she'd brought the children, the baby, the wet nurse and the dog back to her townhouse. She had been greeted by the butler and the housekeeper, who had helped put the children to bed. Mrs. Pots had woken up and demanded to know why the children were there. She had promptly ordered Amelia to bed, saying that they would discuss it the next morning.

Amelia heard the door open and close, but she didn't bother to look at who had come to see her.

Kate came to her side and sat down next to her. "You're up. How are you feeling this morning?"

She said nothing.

"How long have you been crying?"

Wiping her tears, she said, "I don't know. How are the children?"

"They are well, considering what they went through. They're having breakfast. Mrs. Pots is demanding to know why the children are here." Kate stroked Amelia's hair when she didn't reply.

That was going to be a problem. But Amelia couldn't very well have left the children with the townspeople. They needed to be with someone familiar, and she was all they had right now. She'd made it her duty to make sure they were going to be all right.

"I don't know what I am going to tell her." Amelia coughed, and tears came like an unrelenting storm. Shaking her head, she let the tears fall.

"I told Mrs. Pots the children were my cousins."

Amelia looked at Kate, eyes wide. "She believed you?"

"I don't know," Kate said. "But what can she do? This isn't her house, and she is under your employment."

"My grandmother's employment." Oh, the mess she was in now. If her grandmother were here, she would surely murder Amelia.

"I told the woman you were fine with having the children visit. That should give you some time to find homes for them."

They had been home. Now there was nothing left. Surely the earl would be angry about what had transpired last night. Amelia feared what he might say. What he might not say.

Richard may have been right. She was too reckless and too blinded by her own need, and she hadn't considered that others might come to harm. Or she had, and she'd proceeded to ignore the signs because she wanted to fulfill her dreams so badly despite the cost of her terms.

After the girls had come to stay at Somersby Hall, she'd considered educating them and perhaps helping them find their own professions and their own paths. A makeshift school, so to speak, for the girls to learn skills, to read and write. She had mentioned this to Kate, who had thought it was a brilliant idea. Perhaps she would take in a few more children off the streets for a better future.

"What was I thinking?" Amelia said.

"You have a dream, dear friend, a good one."

Amelia looked at her friend. "Had." How could one word fill her with so many emotions? "A dream that nearly destroyed everyone I care about." She paused. "The girls could have been really hurt."

"You could not have known this would happen."

She shook her head. "I should have been more careful. Lord Blackthorn warned me something bad might happen, that I was too reckless. I didn't listen to him. I didn't listen to his warnings."

"Are you saying this was deliberate?"

"I feel it in my bones," she said. "There is a person out there who doesn't want me to be happy."

"You can rebuild," Kate said. "You are the bravest person I know. You wanted the best for those children . . . and Millie. Don't punish yourself like this."

Get a hold of yourself, a voice inside her said. The words she used to tell herself while she was under her grandmother's care, words to bear the torment that woman had put her through.

Kate was right. Sulking in her bed like this was not going to solve her problems. She needed to gather her strength and plan, and inform the earl of the current situation. "You're right, the house can be rebuilt once I am married and I have the funds. All that matters is that the children are safe."

Francis ran into Amelia's room and jumped on her bed, her pudgy face donning a frown, her curls bouncing.

"What is the matter, darling?"

"There is an old woman downstairs. She told me to fetch you."

"Who?" Amelia asked. "Mrs. Pots?"

"No," Francis said. "Some old lady."

Old lady? "Did she say who she was?"

"No, but she was really mad."

"I think we need to get downstairs," Kate said, then picked up the girl and left the room.

Amelia promptly grabbed her robe and put it on. Walking out of her room, she peeked downstairs to see who this old woman was. This mystery woman was standing with a maid. Amelia observed this mystery person from a better angle carefully, then recognition took hold. Oh, my God…

The blood drained from her face.

"Do you think I was pleased when you informed me about my granddaughter's behavior?" the old woman said to Mrs. Pots.

Mrs. Pots frowned. "You wanted me to keep you informed,

so I did as you asked."

"Your job," Amelia's grandmother snapped, "was to make certain my granddaughter didn't make a fool of herself or try to contact her mother."

"I have been in your service for nearly twenty-five years," Mrs. Pots said. "You know how she is. It isn't my fault that she beds the earl like a harlot and sneaks out in the middle of the night."

Oh, no. The woman knew and had said nothing to Amelia.

"Your incompetence is shocking," her grandmother said. "Pack your bag and get out."

Kendall shoved Millie into the bedroom of the small cottage on the outskirts of London. It was a property he had acquired at his gambling hall when a customer didn't have the funds to pay his debt. It was perfect.

"What do ye want from me?" Millie shouted. "I have done nothing to you."

"Shut up," he shouted. "You're lucky I didn't toss you in the Thames with the other whores. I told you not to interfere."

"I didn't," she begged. "Ye told me not to come back, and I didn't come back."

Mrs. Pots walked up to Sir Kendall. "Who is she?"

"Doesn't matter," Sir Kendall said. "You will assist with her delivery," he said to Mrs. Pots, then he pointed to Millie while he continued. "Once that thing is born, I will make certain you never find *it*."

"No," Millie said, sobbing. "Please, don't. I'll leave and never bother ye again. Please."

Kendall said, "I will need you to check up on her. I will return shortly."

"I hope we're not taking her to the Continent with us," Mrs. Pots said.

He'd figure out what to do with Pots later, but for now he needed her to trust him. What a bloody hell. He hated this, all this nonsense. "I need to take care of a few things in London, darling," he said in a soothing tone. "I will be sure to bring something special before we depart." He kissed her on the cheek. "For now, keep an eye on her."

Pots was getting attached to him, and it was starting to annoy him a great deal. And this bloody ordeal with his idiot son wasn't helping him either.

He impatiently walked out of the indistinct cottage and ordered his driver on.

Chapter 30

AMELIA WAS SICK with dizziness.

She faced her grandmother in the parlor, alone. Kate had been asked to take the unruly children and stay out by Amelia's grandmother. And her grandmother's physician had been asked to wait outside.

For a woman who was ill, her grandmother looked awfully healthy. Amelia wouldn't doubt she would live forever.

"Well, what do you have to say for yourself?" her grandmother demanded.

"I did as you asked," she said. "I am engaged to Lord Blackthorn."

"Yes, but it's what you are not saying that is my concern."

What had her chaperone said to her grandmother? The dreadful woman had threatened her multiple times while in London, but she never thought her grandmother would actually come here. *Keep your mouth shut,* she thought.

"Have you lost your tongue?" her grandmother barked. "Speak."

"I did as you asked," Amelia said again.

"Are you sure that is all?"

Her eyes lifted and met her grandmother's shrewd gaze.

"Since you refuse to speak the truth, I will tell you exactly what has reached my ears. You spent the last several weeks reaching out to the very people I ordered you to stay away from. Then, you have gone about late in the evening to God knows where without Mrs. Pots."

Amelia had learned quickly that saying nothing was better than telling her grandmother the truth. *Keep your mouth shut.*

"Has he touched you?" her grandmother demanded. "Are you ruined?"

Amelia jerked in fright. She recalled her last night with Richard, how he had touched her, pleased her. No, this woman could not know the truth.

But before she could answer, her grandmother said, "I thought so. You're no better than your mother."

Amelia kept her eyes lowered as tears brimmed. This couldn't possibly be happening.

Her grandmother sat down on the couch. "Tea," she blurted out.

When the maid peeked in, Amelia said, "Go fetch Lord Blackthorn. Tell him my granddaughter wishes to see him immediately."

"Right away, madam," the maid said.

Fanning her face, she murmured something to herself, clearly irate. "I knew I should have never allowed you to leave Scotland. Nevertheless, you are here and the wedding must happen. Today."

"Today?"

"I managed to procure a special license, so yes, it will happen today." She stopped to catch her breath. "And it will be noted that my will is going to be revised. You will not inherit my money or my properties upon marriage. Instead, the earl will receive a small dowry once you are married."

Amelia's breath caught. Was she not going to be allowed her inheritance? This couldn't be happening. "How small?"

"I will discuss that with the earl," her grandmother snapped. "Once you have produced a child, a healthy one, and that child reaches the age of five, you and the earl will receive my money and properties. If that child dies, you will not inherit a penny."

Five years, Amelia thought with dread. This was not part of the plan. She did not want to have a baby. What would happen to the girls?

The three-legged dog started to bark in the hallway, followed by laughter. The door swung open, and the child ran into the room, the physician chasing them. Francis, carrying the dog, ran straight to Amelia for protection.

"He tried to kick my puppy," Francis said, pointing her finger at the doctor.

"I tried to keep them out, madam."

"Get that filthy animal out of here," the old woman said. "And that unruly child too."

When the physician walked toward them, Amelia leaned in and kissed Francis' forehead. "It's all right. I will be done soon. Go find your sisters." Then Amelia looked at the man and said, "She is quite attached to the dog." She saw that the doctor understood.

Once they left the room, her grandmother narrowed her eyes. "I see that it was a grave mistake to allow you to come here. Grave, grave mistake."

Not only was Amelia to inform the earl his estate had burned down, but now this…

Blackthorn woke to a pounding headache.

Last night, he had visited Zara and thought perhaps another woman might slake his thirst for Amelia.

It hadn't.

Instead, he spent the evening talking to his former mistress about his current predicament and she had listened patiently. Then after an hour, she asked him to leave, that clearly, he needed to think this through on his own.

After, he had gone to a tavern and drank. Then drank some more. What the bloody hell was he getting himself into? What did she mean to him? He was supposed to settle his father's accounts and leave London. Instead, he had been drinking like a drunk, cursing himself.

He couldn't give her what she wanted.

What any woman wanted.

He was incapable of it. He'd known this for a long time, knowing if he didn't die in the field, he'd die alone in peace without attachment to anything or anyone. It was what he had always known his life to be.

You bloody fool.

He sat up on his bed as his valet came into his room. "Miss Knight wishes your presence immediately."

"Immediately?" Blackthorn frowned. What was she up to? Had she discovered relevant information regarding Millie? That must be it; why else would she call on him in such haste?

"Yes, my lord."

"Help me get ready."

It took about fifteen minutes to get dressed, and he skipped breakfast. Stepping out of his London house, he rushed down the street to Amelia's townhouse. It wasn't long before he stepped up the stairs that led to the front door. But even before he could alert the household of his presence, the door swung open.

"Please, come in, my lord," the butler said.

He walked into the quiet foyer, then followed the butler to the parlor. There was a peculiar quiet in this house, one that made him uneasy. When he entered the parlor, he saw Amelia, quiet and with her gaze lowered, sitting next to an unfamiliar older woman and a vicar.

"Lord Blackthorn," the older woman said, standing up to greet him.

"Madam," he said suspiciously, still looking at Amelia. *Has she been crying?* She wouldn't look at him, and in that instant, he suspected this woman may be her grandmother.

"What is going on here?"

Still, Amelia would not look at him.

"Is it not clear?" her grandmother said. "It's your wedding."

"Miss Knight?" he said, looking at her. Still, she said nothing.

"My granddaughter told me everything. So you see, my lord, it is your duty and honor to take proper action."

Dread filled him. "I need to speak with my fiancée. Alone." He was not about to allow this spiteful woman to have her way without speaking to Amelia first. "Everyone out." He saw her grandmother start to protest, but his eyes told her that if she did, she would pay dearly. Once everyone was out and he shut the door, he sat down by Amelia's side and sighed.

"Amelia?" he said softly.

Slowly, she looked up at him, tears dripping down her cheeks.

"Tell me, what is this about?"

She wiped the tears with her finger. "Isn't it obvious? She discovered what I've been up to and now she demands that I marry quickly before it becomes scandalous. She knows about our dalliances."

"I see," he said.

"There is more," she started. "Somersby Hall…"

"What about it?"

"It's destroyed," she said, her voice weak. "Burned down." The last words came out between sobs.

His initial reaction was confusion, but she explained what had happened, and that the girls were safe and with her. Furthermore, she went on to explain that she had meant to inform him of the news, but her grandmother had showed up, having learned of Amelia's actions from Mrs. Pots. In the end, he understood.

But he was angry—at who or what, he wasn't certain.

All he knew was that she could have been hurt, and that troubled him greatly. "I'm happy to hear you and the girls are safe," he said. He was more than happy that she was all right. If anything had happened to her, he would never have forgiven himself for not being there.

"And she changed the terms of the will."

Chapter 31

THIS COULDN'T BE happening. Not under the scrutiny of her grandmother. Amelia had known this day would come, but not like this. And Richard looked quite unhappy. Of course he was—like a prisoner, he had been forced to wed under circumstances that he had not agreed to.

First Somersby Hall and now this?

Richard hadn't spoken a word since the ceremony, when the vicar had congratulated them on their marriage. There had been no joy, no smiles, and no congratulations from friends. It had been efficient and over quickly, as her grandmother wanted.

Still, as he stood there next to her as her husband, he didn't say a single word. And the expression on his face worried her deeply. Did he regret this?

She didn't want this. Not like this. Any kind of emotion would do. At least she knew how he felt. Well, she knew he wasn't happy, but honestly, he could at least acknowledge he wasn't happy. That she could live with. Anything but this silence.

But, in truth, they had said everything they had to say, with dread.

"Do I need to stay to make sure the marriage is consummated?" her grandmother said.

"There is no need for that," Amelia said.

"Good," she said.

Her grandmother's doctor insisted she should rest, so she went upstairs with her physician to retire. Kate and the children had not been permitted to attend the wedding as her grandmother hadn't wished it.

"I am sorry about all this. I know this isn't the plan you agreed to," Amelia said to Richard once they were alone.

He said nothing.

"Can you at least say something?"

"What else is there to say?" he said. "The deed is done."

"So, then, are we going to live out the rest of our lives without speaking with one another?"

"I have to go, to think."

"You do?" she said. "You regret this?"

"I didn't say that," he replied. "I just need to think."

With that, he walked out of the parlor and left her alone, shattering her heart to pieces.

Walking down the steps to the street, Blackthorn exhaled.

What was this strange ache in his heart? This confusion that seemed to plague him? He wasn't certain what this was. It was not as if he spent his days contemplating his emotions. That kind of luxury was not for him. He didn't have the time or the need, as his former occupation hadn't allowed him that kind of indulgence.

But he'd given up on that profession.

Why did he want to leave London? Granted, the only memories he had of this place were the shouts and screams of his parents to each other when he had visited them. He had dreaded the visits to Blackthorn Hall. Was that the reason?

Yes, he had learned to numb himself when they fought like cats and dogs. He and his brother, Max, used to hide in his room and they comforted each other when the fight would last for hours, doors slamming.

Screams.

Broken vases.

And blood . . .

The things his parents used to say to each other, spiteful comments and verbal abuse—that was what he remembered the most.

And tears. Not his mother's tears. His father's silent tears. He'd only been seven years old and he could remember it like it was yesterday. She'd often leave and find comfort with her lover while his father locked himself up for days in his study. She would not return for weeks. Until finally she left them for good.

He felt the unpleasant sensation growing deep in the pit of his gut. God, he felt like he was seven again, like that damn boy who used to cover his ears with his hands to block out the hell that was his reality.

The carriage door in front of him opened and out came Philip.

Blackthorn stopped in his tracks. "What are you doing here?"

"We need to talk, privately." Philip motioned for Blackthorn to join him in the carriage. Once they were ensconced in the carriage, Philip spoke again. "I need your help. I must confess I cannot do this myself as it involves my father."

"Continue," Blackthorn said.

"I think my father has kidnapped Millie. She is carrying my child. I don't know what he plans to do with her or my child, but he can be quite cruel when he is angry, and I fear for her life."

"Be a man," he said. "You must confront your father."

"How can I?" Philip said. "He is all I've got."

"That is the precise reason you need to." Blackthorn heard his own words, and something in him clicked. He knew what he needed to do. What he must do.

"I can't."

"I will accompany you," he said softly. "You must do this; otherwise, Millie will never forgive you, and you may never see your child."

Philip looked at Blackthorn, his face dour and uncertain, his eyes frightened. "I will go with you."

Chapter 32

SIR KENDALL MUST have been pacing for hours; he was starting to give himself a headache.

He wanted this damn child here, so he could get on with his plan.

How had he gotten into this mess? Or rather, his idiot son had gotten him into this mess. The decision to burn that damn house, Somersby Hall, had been a risky one, but it had given him great joy to see it burn.

So much so that it had given him an idea.

He'd take the baby with him if it was a boy. Philip could raise the damn child and raise him properly. As for Pots and Millie, he planned on getting rid of them permanently. Philip should be pleased enough to keep his mouth shut and it would give him something to focus on while they were in Italy.

There was a knock on the door. He pulled the heavy curtain aside and peeked out the front window. Good, she was here.

When he opened the door, Pots entered. Putting her bag by her feet, she embraced Kendall, sobbing. *What is wrong with this damn woman?* "Dry your tears. The baby is coming."

Mrs. Pots wiped her cheeks and lifted her bag to place it on a chair before heading into the room where the cry of a soon-to-be mother was heard.

Amelia was still sitting in the parlor, stunned and numb.

She wouldn't blame Richard if he despised her now. He had been forced into a union without a voice and into a plan he hadn't agreed to. Somersby Hall was gone, and Richard would not get the inheritance for who knew how many years. What if Amelia was barren and couldn't have children? What if, what if, what if?

Kate quietly entered the parlor and sat down next to her. "The children and the baby are all in their room. The nurse has them."

"Good," Amelia said.

"Where is Lord Blackthorn?" Kate asked.

"He said he needed to think," she said.

"Think about what?"

"He didn't say," she replied.

Kate watched her, careful before she spoke. "I am certain he just needs a little bit of time to adjust."

"Perhaps," Amelia said. "I won't blame him if he decides he wants an annulment once my grandmother returns home."

"I doubt that," she said. "He would have stopped the ceremony if he didn't care about you."

"Do you think so?" Amelia said with hope. Still, if he had cared for her, she doubted he did so now. Goodness, he had looked positively angry, as if he would have been ready to thrash her grandmother if she weren't a woman. One thing was certain, the man had control.

"Give it time," Kate said. "You can rebuild Somersby Hall once you inherit."

"I don't know. Everything has gone wrong ever since I arrived here. Nothing has worked out the way I planned. And I still don't know where Millie may be. Maybe this is a sign." There was a moment of silence, and Kate waited patiently for Amelia to continue, but she had nothing to say. Nothing worth mentioning, and she was emotionally tired.

"What will you do?"

She shook her head. "I don't know."

"What will you do with the children?"

"I haven't thought of that yet. I so want them to remain together . . . with me, but—"

"They can stay with me," Kate said. "At least until you can figure out what to do with them."

"I can't ask you to do that."

"The children are part of you," Kate said. "And you are part of my life. They can stay with me. Besides, it will do me some good to fill that hideously big castle with some laugher."

"Oh, thank you, thank you." She beamed. "From the bottom of my heart, thank you, Kate."

"Now, let's get some fresh air."

Both women stood up from the couch and walked out of the parlor to the foyer.

"Why don't we go for a stroll at Bond Street, hmm?" Kate suggested.

Kate kicked something, and a crumpled piece of paper rolled a foot away. She picked it up and smoothed it out. They both looked at it with interest.

13 Sheen Lane, London

"What could this mean?" Amelia said.

"I don't know," Kate said. "Shall we find out?"

"We can't," Amelia said. "We don't know whose property this is. Besides, what about the children?"

"The nurse is with them and the housekeeper is here."

Amelia sighed, knowing she wasn't going to get anything done here. And with her grandmother resting upstairs, she felt trapped. Utterly trapped.

"All right, let's find out."

Chapter 33

"WHEN IS THE bloody baby coming?" Kendall muttered to himself, pacing in the parlor. Mrs. Pots was still in the bedroom with Millie, with agonizing screams coming from the room.

The baby finally came after nearly ten hours of labor. Mrs. Pots walked into the parlor with an infant in her arms, a smile on her face as she ogled at the baby. "It's a boy . . . a little boy."

"Good," he replied.

"Where are you going?"

"I need to fetch my boy," Kendall said. He needed to get the baby away from this madwoman. She actually thought she was going to keep the baby.

"Shall I wait for you with the baby?"

"No," he said. "I have a wet nurse waiting for him. She's at my London home. Once I deliver the baby there, I will come for you, so be ready. I don't want Millie causing any more trouble, so keep her quiet." He had no plans to fetch anyone once he left with the baby.

The ship would sail at first light, so they needed to get to Portsmouth to depart for Italy.

"Give me the baby," he said. Just then, he heard a shrill cry from Millie in the bedroom. "Keep her quiet."

Reluctantly, Mrs. Pots gave the baby to Kendall. "You will come back soon?"

"Of course, darling. Just be ready."

He walked out of the parlor and down the hall to the foyer. Stepping into the darkness, he closed the door behind him. The quiet of the night was refreshing, and the sounds of nature somehow soothed the tension mounting in his neck. A sudden noise in the distant thick oak trees beyond the farmland caught his attention. He looked in that direction and narrowed his eyes. Reaching into his coat, he felt the pistol there.

Taking no risks, he walked up to his carriage parked nearby and placed the baby on the seat. When he looked up to tell his driver that he was ready, he noticed his driver was missing.

Where the hell are you? He must be relieving himself. Kendall grabbed his pistol. He waited a few seconds longer, looking around the periphery of the property.

Nothing. No sound.

No driver.

Footfalls alerted him. From this distance, it was difficult to see the person approaching. "Approach slowly," he said, lifting his pistol, just to be cautious.

Then he saw the approaching man's face.

He froze—oh, bloody fucking hell.

Chapter 34

THIS WASN'T THE first time Blackthorn had had a pistol directed right at him. The moon was bright above him, giving Kendall a clear view.

"Step away," Kendall said. He slowly positioned himself so that the open field was at his back. One, two, three. He stepped backward, not taking the pistol off Blackthorn.

"There's nowhere to go," Blackthorn said.

"Do not attempt to follow me. I would hate for something to happen to your mother."

Blackthorn stopped in his tracks, hands in the air. While he may have his disagreements with his mother, he didn't want to see her hurt.

"Do you really think I would be that mindless as to let you direct me any way you please?" Kendall said. "If harm comes to me, young man, I have arranged to have your family shame on the front page of The London Times. . . the whores—he had a taste for them, a little more than what was good for him, if you know what I mean."

French pox. That explained the erratic behavior Blackthorn had witnessed before his father passed. Still, he was not going to bite. "It's over. Drop the pistol before someone gets hurt."

"As you command, my lord," he jested with a grimace. "Who do you think you are speaking to?"

Kendall backed away slowly. Blackthorn didn't. If Kendall ran into the woods, finding him was going to be difficult.

"Put the pistol down—"

Kendall aimed and pulled the trigger. A loud bang followed. Richard felt the wind from the bullet passing his head. Bloody hell.

By the time he regained his focus, Kendall was already diving into the woods. Blackthorn followed, and before he had the chance the shield himself in the thick of the trees, Kendall shot at him again. This time, the bullet grazed Blackthorn's upper arm with a sharp, cutting pain.

"Give up, young man," Kendall shouted as Blackthorn kept his pace steady.

Once he was in the thick of the woods, everything stilled. He stopped. His eyes adjusted to the darkness, the light of the moon giving him some visibility.

Then footfalls.

Crunch. Snap.

He followed the subtle sound, listening. Right. No, left. He heard the snap of a twig to his right again, so he quickly followed, picking up his pace. Then, from the periphery, he saw a figure running a few yards from him.

Blackthorn took off in a sprint, then lunged at Kendall,

and both men fell to the leafy ground with a thump. Kendall screamed in agony. Blackthorn wrestled the pistol out of his hand and threw it.

"You're going to live a long, miserable life in prison, I will make sure of that."

Kendall spit in his face. "Not if I have anything to do about—"

Bam.

Crack. Thump.

With Blackthorn's punch, Kendall was knocked out. Blackthorn lowered himself and looked at Kendall. "You are going to pay, I will make certain of that, old man."

Blackthorn grabbed Kendall by the collar, dragged him out of the woods, and dropped him near the cottage like a bag of rubbish.

The Bow Street Runner, Kane Roberts, approached. "I got your note and arrived as fast as I could."

"Good, I was worried you wouldn't get my note in time."

"I'll escort him to Bow Street," Roberts said. "I've already informed the Magistrate regarding this matter."

"Thank you," Blackthorn said.

The sound of a carriage alerted them. "Are you expecting anyone?"

The runner shook his head. "This should be interesting."

The carriage came to a full halt, and the door opened. Amelia and Kate stepped out of the carriage. What the bloody hell were they doing here? From the expression on the runner's face, clearly he didn't have a clue either.

"What are you two doing here?" Blackthorn asked.

Amelia approached him. "We found this in the foyer of my London house." She handed him the crumpled note with the address. "What is this place?"

A baby wailed in the waiting carriage, and their heads turned toward the sound. Amelia ran to the carriage and inside she saw a baby. Picking up the infant, she faced the others. "What is going on here?"

Just then, Mrs. Pots opened the cottage door. "What are you doing with that baby?" she said, running to her. "He is my baby."

My God, the woman was mad. And why was Mrs. Pots here? Kate quickly stopped Mrs. Pots from reaching for the baby. "What are you doing here? And where is the baby's mother?"

Mrs. Pots looked toward the house, but she seemed afraid to speak.

"Is the mother of this baby inside?"

When the baby wailed, Mrs. Pots looked at him. "He needs me."

"He needs his mother," Amelia said, her voice softening. As much as she hated the woman, Mrs. Pots had suffered too under the scrutiny of Amelia's grandmother.

"Because of you, my daughter lost everything," Mrs. Pots said spitefully.

Lost everything? Amelia was confused. "What does she have to do with this? Your daughter is happily married."

"To a farmer," Mrs. Pots snapped. "A poor man with nothing to show for it. My daughter was promised a part of the inheritance until you showed up and the old woman changed her will."

Amelia had met Mrs. Pots' daughter a few times, but she had not been aware of this promise.

Mrs. Pots added, "I was the only loyal friend and companion she had, and my daughter worshiped her."

"It was not my doing. I had no wish to take your daughter's place, and I certainly didn't want to stay with my grandmother, you know this," Amelia said patiently. She understood Mrs. Pots' suffering now, why she'd hated Amelia all these years. But that didn't mean she could treat everyone here the way she pleased.

Mrs. Pots' tears dripped down slowly. "I sacrificed everything for that woman."

"I know," Amelia said. "We all have."

The woman looked at the baby again. "I had nothing to do with the fire. You have to believe me," she said desperately. "I told him not to do it. I told him it was a bad idea. He didn't want to listen to me."

Amelia patiently nodded. The baby started to wail louder. "I know," she said softly. "The baby needs her mother . . . *he* needs to feed. I am going to take the baby inside now."

"Go," Blackthorn said. "Millie should be inside."

Chapter 35

AMELIA RAN INSIDE holding the infant in her arms, calling out Millie's name, with Kate following her. Walking up the stairs, she called out for her friend. Kate went ahead to check the rooms.

In a few seconds, she heard Kate calling her. Following her voice, she walked down the narrow hall and saw a door ajar. She entered with the baby in her arms.

There she saw Kate untying the rope wrapped around Millie, who had been positioned most disturbingly in the corner of the room. Amelia's heart throbbed in anticipation as Kate removed the gag in Millie's mouth. She gently handed the baby to Kate and hugged Millie tightly in her arms, tears falling like a storm.

Sickness came over her at the thought of her friend in fear, not knowing if she would live or die. Millie was in tattered clothes that looked as though she hadn't changed them in years. And her once-bouncy gold-blond curls were in dirty knots. Her eyes were barely open, and she looked so fragile . . . so thin.

Amelia said in a shaky voice, "Oh, Millie, I am so sorry."

"Amelia?" Millie said, her voice hoarse. Her lips were cracked and dry.

"Yes, it's me. Shh . . . don't speak now. We'll get a physician to look you over."

"I kept my promise," Millie barely said.

"Oh, what promise?" Amelia said, wiping the tears on Millie's cheeks.

"I didn't steal from the baker after you left. I kept my promise."

Tears poured down Amelia's cheeks. "That's wonderful. Oh, Millie. I am so sorry." Her voice rumbled, choked with tears. "I should have come for you when you wrote," she said. "I'm sorry it took so long to keep my promise to you, Millie."

Millie smiled. "I am glad I got to see you again."

Wiping her tears on her sleeves, Amelia hugged Millie. "I will never leave you again. You are going home with me."

Chapter 36

AMELIA WATCHED AS Kate, Millie, and Millie's infant rode away in her carriage. She'd promised to join them soon. Kane Roberts had apprehended Kendall and Mrs. Pots and taken them to Bow Street where they would be kept in a cell to face charges in court.

Mrs. Pots had begged to be forgiven and said that she had been coerced into helping him. Part of Amelia wanted to forgive, but if Mrs. Pots had helped kidnap her friend, there was nothing Amelia could do to help her now.

As much as she hated this, she needed to face Richard. To give him a way out of their situation if he desired it. It wasn't fair for him to be forced into an arrangement he hadn't agreed to. It was time to face her grandmother and tell her exactly what she should have said from the beginning.

She would have to face the reality after. If she had to wash dishes for a living, she would do it, but if Kate could help her until she could find a proper job, perhaps as a governess, she could help Millie and her child.

Yes, that sounded like a good plan. The only problem was she would dearly miss Richard. More than miss him. She would be heartbroken, but it would have to be if he wished it. She wouldn't be able to live with herself if he chose to stay because he felt he had been forced into it. It was the least she could do; after all, she had approached him to propose the idea.

Once the carriages were out of sight, she strolled to him. The grimace on his face was hard to endure, but this could not wait.

"May I take you home?" he asked.

She nodded. He helped her into his carriage and he joined her, sitting across from her. It reminded her of the night he had rescued them in the alley. The way he had risked his life to help a stranger. Even the expression on his face made it difficult to speak. After all, they hadn't spoken since the wedding, when he'd rushed out.

"I want to thank you for everything you've done," she said softly.

He gave her a slight smile, one that helped ease the tension somehow. Oh, how she wanted to kiss him and tell him how much she appreciated him and all that he'd done for her. She wanted to kiss him first thing in the morning and between meals, and she wanted him to be the last person she saw before bed. Oh, how she loved him.

She loved him?

Yes, she loved him.

And this was going to be a more-than-difficult conversation to have. "I think it is only fair that we get an annulment."

"Annulment?" he said, frowning. "What about the inheritance?"

"I realized after seeing Millie that this life is short, and I don't wish to live under my grandmother's scrutiny any longer. If I have to, I will find an occupation, something I can do to earn a living."

"You've thought this through, haven't you?"

"I have," she said. "Governess would be a good occupation for me. It makes sense, since I never wanted to be married or have children." She paused and looked nervously at her hands. "Of course, this means you won't get your part of the inheritance, which I am sorry for. If I had it, I'd give it to you. You've done more than you promised, but I haven't. You've lost Somersby Hall because of me."

Why was he looking at her as if he were about to toss her out of the carriage? Was he angry that he wasn't going to get his money? To make things worse, he wasn't saying anything to make this easier on her.

"I guess that's it," she said. "I plan to leave soon. The sooner the better, actually. And you will be free to choose another heiress, one that has something to offer you. I am sure there are plenty in London Society."

"Sounds like a good plan," he said.

Her heart sank. He could at least pretend to be disappointed. "It is, isn't it?" she said, her tone suddenly perking up. She was beginning to get angry as his indifference. After all they'd shared, how could he? She looked out the window, frowning. Ugh, she hated when he got to her like this. "And by the way, I don't—"

He cut her off with, "You're angry with me."

"You're right, I am."

"Why?"

"I don't want to say. It's over between us. Besides, you would not understand."

"Try me."

She opened her mouth and saw that he was ginning. "Are you laughing at me? This isn't amusing, not to me."

He shifted and sat next to her. "My foolish wife, I always love that spark of yours."

My wife? Her heart started to beat against her chest faster and faster. "I don't understand. You were so angry with me after the wedding."

"I did need to think things through," he said. "To figure out what this is between us."

"And what is this?" she said, not realizing she was holding her breath in anticipation.

"I don't know," he confessed. "All I know is my life seems unfit without you. I can't imagine you not in it. I can't imagine waking up without you next to me. I want you with me permanently."

She was relieved and happy. Very happy. Tears fell as the weight of sorrow she'd been carrying in her heart from losing him left her. "How could you just sit there and watch me make a fool of myself?"

He grabbed her hands in his and kissed her fingers.

"What about the money? You won't get my inheritance straightaway. What about leaving London? The annulment?" she asked.

"I'd rather have the woman I love, if you don't mind."

She gasped in surprise. "You love me?"

"I do, deeply. I suppose I have since the day we met."

She lunged and wrapped her arms around him, and they both fell back onto the seat. "Oh, Richard. I thought I was going to lose you," she said, weeping.

"I was an idiot. I realized why I hated this place as much as I did. Why I kept running. Why I joined the army."

"Why did you run?" She searched his eyes, and there was sadness there. "It's all right if you don't want to discuss it."

"I do, actually," he said with a sigh. "My parents were, I was told, madly in love. So much so, everyone was jealous of their union because they were so happy together. I recall the fights started when I was four, maybe five. They fought relentlessly, but that wasn't what made me stay away. I could deal with shouts and angry exchanges, but it was my brother's crying that really got to me. He'd sob and wonder when our mother was coming back. He was never the same after she finally left us, and she didn't return. With my mother gone, my father took to drinking more and more and whoring. I left to travel the world spying for my country, not really having a home, nor missing it. I didn't want the responsibility of a family or to take the chance of repeating what my parents and my brother and I went through. It was hell for everyone. To be perfectly honest, I didn't want to be trapped here and be faced with hating someone for the choices I made because it was expected of me. I liked my freedom and I didn't want to give it up."

She saw the melancholy on his face and she wanted to

soothe his sorrow, but she gave him the space he needed to say what he had to say to her.

"I came home when my brother passed. My mother didn't come to his funeral even after my father begged for her presence. What kind of mother does that to her own child?"

Amelia's heart broke as she listened to his story. What kind of a mother does this? She had thought the same thing when her mother gave her up and never came to visit her or wrote to her, so she understood that pain. "I don't know why she did what she did, but I will always be there for you, I promised you this."

He kissed her and smiled. "I know. But know that I'm not telling you this for sympathy, but just so you'll understand that my view on marriage isn't what it ought to be." He paused to look at her. "But I also know I don't want to live without you next to me."

Her heart soared and broke for his suffering. "Oh, my love, I will never leave your side. Trust me on this." She smiled and wrapped her arms around him. "I won't, my love."

"Even when I'm in a foul mood?"

"No, you fool. And if you want to leave London, or England for that matter, I will be by your side wherever you want to go."

"What about the children, the baby?"

Her eyes widened. "Does that mean we can have them with us?"

"If that is what you want."

"I do, I wish to educate them. Perhaps we can even start a school for these girls once I inherit. We can rebuild. And travel too."

He smiled and caressed her cheek. "A good plan, my wife," he said.

Epilogue

Blackthorn Hall
Five days later...

"OUR FAMILY IS owed an inheritance. That was the arrangement," Richard's mother said.

Richard's mother had been ecstatic when he and Amelia told her the news of their wedding, and she had decided to throw a grand ball in honor of their union, but Richard had informed her there wouldn't be a ball, that her account would be frozen, and she would be given a monthly allowance to live on. It had taken her a moment to comprehend Richard's words, but once she did, she was irate, to say the least.

"This is ridiculous. The only reason my son married you was for your money."

"Enough," Richard ordered, his tone echoing throughout the parlor, making his mother go silent in shock. "You will not say such things to my wife. Do you understand?"

"How dare you? I am your mother—"

"Where were you when Max was asking for you as a child? Where were you when Father asked you to come to your son's funeral? Where were you when he was ill and wrote to you to reconcile?"

She opened her mouth to respond, but quickly shut it.

"You will have a comfortable life and an allowance, but if you are not satisfied with the living that I have provided for you *because* you are still my mother after all the suffering you have caused, you may go back to your lover."

Her jaw twitched, and her eyes narrowed at her son and Amelia. "Welcome to the family, my dear." This was all she said, and she retired to her room.

Philip had wed Millie Penn privately with a special license he had procured for them that morning. They had decided to retire to Philip's London townhouse for some privacy for a few days as their honeymoon, while Amelia had offered to look after their baby. They had named him Henry.

Despite the news that Sir Kendall would be on trial for several counts of attempted murder and was being held in prison, Philip seemed to be in good spirits. Millie and several witnesses had all come forward and made their statements to the Justice in London.

Amelia wasn't a fool. She understood what it felt like to lose a parent, and it was always painful, despite their shortcomings. A few times, she saw Philip staring into space, thinking. His expression had been melancholy, but there was nothing she could say to him that would help ease his heart. It would come with time, she surmised, as it had for her.

Francis ran into the room, followed by Kate, who was

carrying the baby, and the other five girls, quickly filling up the room. A few seconds later, the three-legged dog ran into the room, wagging its tail and barking. Francis quickly scooped the dog up in her arms and ran to Amelia.

"What is it, darling?"

"They are taking over my life."

"Taking over your life?"

"They said I can't name my puppy Balls."

"That is a silly name," Beatrice, the oldest sibling, said. "You can't name it Balls."

"It looks like a fur ball to me, so I can."

The butler knocked and entered. "There is someone here for you, Miss Knight. I mean, my lady."

"Oh?" Amelia asked. "Who is it?"

"Mr. Hendrickson," he said.

"Do you want me to see to this person?" her husband asked, coming to her side.

"I can see to it, thank you," she said, kissing him with a wide smile.

"I will go with you," Richard said.

When the visitor was invited into Richard's study, he sat down in front of Richard, and the new countess next to him. Mr. Hendrickson had come with the news that her grandmother had passed away on her way back to Scotland during the night at one of the inns.

Her grandmother had departed London the morning after the wedding. She had looked pale, and her doctor had informed her it would be best to rest for a few more days before heading home. She had refused, stating that if she was going to die, she'd rather do it in her own bed.

Mr. Hendrickson apologized for not getting there sooner, but he'd had to finish up some business matters in London.

"Your grandmother, Elise Knight has left you everything," Mr. Hendrickson said.

It took a moment for Amelia to fully grasp what he was saying. "There must be a mistake. My grandmother indicated to me that I would inherit only if I produced an offspring," Amelia said.

"I went over the entire document signed by your grandmother before traveling here."

A whirl of emotions rumbled inside her. She was overjoyed with the news of her inheritance, but the knowledge that her grandmother had died hit her hard. Despite the torture the woman had put her through, she was the only living member of her family. She had wished, oh, so wished they could bond in a way that they never had.

"What is the matter?" Richard asked, watching her expression.

"I just need a moment." This meant she could rebuild Somersby Hall. To build the place, a school for the girls they'd taken under their wing.

Soon after, Blackthorn escorted the secretary out. When he opened the door, a woman was standing there, her hand poised by the knocker.

"May I help you?" Blackthorn asked.

"I was told Amelia Knight was here."

Blackthorn observed the woman with curiosity. "Who

might you be?"

"I am sorry," the stranger said, as if embarrassed by her lack of social courtesy. "My name is Mrs. Ryan."

"My darling, who is here?" Amelia said, smiling. He widened the door and Amelia stopped dead in her tracks, shock apparent on her face, her expression tight and hard.

"Hello, Amelia," the woman said, studying Amelia's face.

Say something, her mind ordered. Sprinkles of gray spotted the woman's dark brown hair. And there were winkles, a lot more of them than Amelia recalled.

"How are you familiar with my wife?" Richard said.

"She is my mother," Amelia finally answered for her mother, the woman who had abandoned her. How dare she show up after all these years? Amelia watched her expression. There was sadness in her eyes. Perhaps life had been continuously difficult for her.

"I'm sorry. Maybe coming here was a bad idea," Mrs. Ryan reluctantly said.

"Would you like to come in?" Richard said, intervening.

Mrs. Ryan looked at Amelia curiously, then at her daughter's husband. When Amelia didn't protest, the woman entered, and Richard closed the door behind them.

"Thank you," Mrs. Ryan said.

All three walked in silence to the parlor, and Richard invited her to sit. Amelia was tormented by the unsaid words. How could her mother show up after all these years? Did she want money? Why was she here?

"It's a lovely house," the woman said, sitting down.

"Why are you here?" Amelia asked, her tone curt and irritated. "I've done just fine without you for a decade. I hope you aren't thinking to ask me for money." Amelia wondered what had happened to her mother to have given her so much grief.

"Is that why you think I am here?"

"Isn't it?" she said. "You haven't written. Not a single word and you show up now?"

Mrs. Ryan frowned, her brows drawing together in confusion. "You didn't receive the letters?"

"What letters?" Was it possible that she had a heart in there somewhere? That she did care about her only child?

Her mother's eyes brimmed with angry tears. "I should have known she would not allow you to have them."

"What letters?"

"I sent you a letter on your birthday each year. They weren't returned so I assumed you received them."

Amelia let out a heavy sigh, tears falling. There was a feeling of relief, her resentment slowly fading away. All these years of wondering why her mother had abandoned her. Why she never came to visit. But in fact, her mother cared.

"Why don't I give you two some privacy," Richard said, kissing Amelia on the temple, his eyes filled with love. "Come get me when you are ready."

"No, wait," she said, grabbing his hand to hold him. "I want you here, darling." She looked at her mother. "Why did you not come to visit me?"

"When your grandmother agreed to take care of you,

she informed me that if I made any attempt to visit you, she would make sure you were sent straightaway to the workhouse."

A sense of strength came to Amelia, and her anger slowly started to fade away. But there were questions she needed answers to. "How could you give up your own child?"

Her mother wiped the tears on her cheek. "It's a choice that is impossible for any mother to live with. I can't justify giving you up. The only thing I can say is that I thought she could give you what I could not. A roof over your head. Hot meals. A warm blanket. A future I could not give you."

Amelia's lips quivered with happiness.

Her mother smiled. "Millie wrote to me about you and Lord Blackthorn. I came to congratulate you." She paused. "And . . . to see your face again after all these years."

Amelia went to her mother and looked into her eyes. There was a lingering sorrow in them, so compelling and heartfelt. They embraced for a long while.

When they parted, her mother wiped her tears and looked at Richard. "My congratulations to you, my lord."

"Richard," he said. "After all, I am your son-in-law."

Amelia touched the stone on her silver necklace. "I never took this off."

Her mother's eyes sparkled with tears. "I saw you wearing it." She smiled, touching the stone and caressing it between her fingers. "Your father gave this to me on our wedding day." Tears trickled down her cheeks. Wiping them away, she said, "He was a good man and he loved you so very much. Despite your grandmother blaming me for ruining his future and disowning him, he gave us so much love. You have his compassion, his heart. When he passed, your grandmother became angry with me, with the world. She blamed me for ruining her family."

Amelia's heart swelled with joy. "I know. She reminded me often. There were times I wanted nothing to do with this necklace, but it was the only thing I had that Grandmamma allowed me to keep."

"How is she? I hope she treated you well."

Ten years of abuse flashed through her mind, but it had all been worth it because she had the man she loved, the children, and her mum now. "She passed recently."

Her mother wiped her tears of joy. "You have a brother," Mrs. Ryan said, her eyes still filled with endless tears. "His name is James. He is five. I wanted to have more, but my husband insists that one is enough for us, considering my health."

"You're ill?"

"After I had James, it took quite a while for me to recover my strength. Nearly a year."

Amelia had lived with the belief that she was not worthy, having been given away and living under constant threat. She had honestly believed that she could not trust anyone, and that she didn't deserve happiness. But Richard had opened her heart. Amelia understood the need for acceptance, despite our flaws, and to learn to trust those we love, to forgive others for ourselves. She had learned this at a price, but it was worth every pain, every minute. And now, she was reunited with her mother, she thought with delight.

Her family, and the girls, were all complete.

"Would you like to stay for dinner?" Amelia asked.

Her mother's eyes gleamed with tears and she nodded. "Very much."

"I'd like to meet James. And your husband."

"He is a good man, like your father. You remind me of him."

There was a quick knock and Richard gave his permission to enter. The door swung open. "My Lord, there is a U.S. Marshal here to see you."

"U.S. Marshal?" he said.

Amelia and Richard looked at each other, perplexed. What would a United States Marshal be doing here? This day was proving to bring one surprise after another.

"What would you like me to tell him, my lord?"

Amelia and Richard walked past the butler to the front door and opened it. A tall man stood there wearing a trench coat that reached midway to his dirty boots. He wore a brimmed hat reminiscent of a cowboy in the Wild West.

"Pardon me, madam, but I am looking for Mrs. Kate McBride."

"And who might you be?"

"Jonathan Hawk, U.S. Marshal. I am told Mrs. McBride resides here."

"She does," Amelia said. "But I must ask, what is the urgency of this matter? We have guests."

The man seemed reluctant to say, so when she insisted he answer her question, he said to her, "Is she here or not?"

"No need to be rude, Mr. Hawk."

Just then Kate walked in to join them. Everyone turned to look at her, and the blood drained from Kate's face, leaving her pale.

"You," Kate said. "What are *you* doing here?"

"To make sure you stand trial for murder."

I hope you enjoyed Sinful Pleasures.

Want More?

Sinful Kiss

(Book 2 of Sinful Ladies of London Novel)
Coming soon…

For updates, bonus content and giveaways,
sign up for my newsletter: www.kristijun.com

Join me on my Facebook Page to stay connected:
https://bit.ly/2Idj4WA

Facebook Reader Group (closed group):
https://bit.ly/2rAYnxy

You will get my future books for FREE (Advance Reader
Copy – ARC) when you join my Facebook Review Team
(closed group): https://bit.ly/2qrMDN5

Happy Reading!
Kristi

About the Author

Kristi Jun resides in Southern California with her infinitely patient husband, and beautiful quirky son and two goofy Australian Labradoodles. If she isn't conjuring up another happily-ever-after, she can be found searching for the web for all things English, watching reruns of Star Trek, Dr. Who, and Downton Abbey.

Made in the USA
Columbia, SC
10 November 2018